How Our Government Built America,
and Why It Must Rebuild Now

BOLD ENDEAVORS

Felix Rohatyn

SIMON & SCHUSTER
New York   London   Toronto   Sydney

Simon & Schuster
1230 Avenue of the Americas
New York, NY 10020

First Simon & Schuster hardcover edition February 2009

SIMON & SCHUSTER and colophon are registered trademarks
of Simon & Schuster, Inc.

For information about special discounts for bulk purchases,
please contact Simon & Schuster Special Sales at
1-800-456-6798 or business@simonandschuster.com.

Designed by Jaime Putorti

Manufactured in the United States of America

10 9 8 7 6 5 4 3 2 1

Library of Congress Cataloging-in-Publication Data
Rohatyn, Felix G., 1928–
    Bold endeavors / Felix Rohatyn.
        p.   cm.
    1. Infrastructure (Economics)—Government policy—United States.   2. Public
works—United States.   3. Public investments—United States.   4. United States—
Social policy—1993–   I. Title.
    HC110.C3R57   2009
    388.0973—dc22

                                                                                            2008053009

ISBN-13: 978-1-4165-3312-2
ISBN-10:   1-4165-3312-5

For Elizabeth
With all love

CONTENTS

Contents

— SEVEN —

The Rural Electrification Administration *133*

— EIGHT —

The Reconstruction Finance Corporation *153*

— NINE —

The G.I. Bill *179*

— TEN —

The Interstate Highway System *199*

BOLD
ENDEAVORS

PROLOGUE

THE NATION IS FALLING apart—literally. America's roads and bridges, schools and hospitals, airports and railways, ports and dams, waterlines and air-control systems—the country's entire infrastructure—is rapidly and dangerously deteriorating.

When the levees fail to hold back the floodwaters in New Orleans or a bridge collapses during rush hour in Minneapolis, there are headlines and collective national sighs of concern. Short-term solutions are offered up. But after the sense of emergency passes, the country's attention moves on, too. These tragedies, however, are only harbingers of the many national disasters that are to come.

Time has taken its toll on America. Consider these daunting

statistics cited in a recent report to Congress: Three quarters of the country's public school buildings are outdated and inadequate. More than a quarter of the nation's bridges are obsolete or deficient. It will take $11 billion *annually* to replace aging drinking water facilities. Half the locks on the more than 12,000 miles of inland waterways are functionally obsolete. The American Society of Civil Engineers has estimated that over the next five years an investment of $1.6 *trillion* will be needed simply to make the nation's infrastructure dependable and safe.

Worse, while little is being done to remedy these deficiencies, the demands on the nation's beleaguered infrastructure continue to grow. Over the next decade airline passenger travel is anticipated to increase by about one third. Freight tonnage will grow by nearly one half. And the highways and roads will continue to be clogged: Americans already spend 3.5 billion hours each year in traffic.

Greater demand multiplied by increased deterioration is an equation that can only produce woeful results for the nation. Aviation delays will cost the U.S. economy an estimated $30 billion by 2015. Traffic congestion will waste untold hours, further pollute the air, and burn nearly $100 billion each year in wasted fuel. More consequentially, each year an estimated 13,000 deaths can be attributed to poor highway maintenance.

There are, of course, many other disturbing examples of decay throughout the country that could be cited in this equation. Ports, trains, schools, waste and water systems—the nation is growing older on every front. Regardless of what is scrutinized, in the end it all adds up to the same very despairing result: The aging of our nation's infrastructure has lessened our productivity, undermined our ability to compete in the global economy, shaken our perceptions about our own safety and health, and damaged the quality of American life.

What must be done?

America needs to rebuild its infrastructure. It is a critical national priority, a costly long-term investment, and a visionary enterprise. It is a program that can provide tens of millions of much needed jobs. And it is an undertaking that can only succeed if it is directed, coordinated, and largely financed by the federal government.

THIS BOOK IS AN attempt to demonstrate through ten examples from our history that the federal government has traditionally been the indispensable investor in our nation. Each of the ten chapters is a case study of how an activist government, led by bold leaders with vision and perseverance, made far-seeing investments that helped to shape America. Presidents Jefferson, Lincoln, and Franklin Roosevelt, in fact, heroically found the will in the midst of grave national crises to look beyond the turmoil of the times in which they lived to strengthen the nation's future. Together, these ten historical precedents offer up a balance sheet of sorts: an accounting of the many returns, anticipated and unanticipated, material and spiritual, that the nation has reaped from propitious government investments—decisions which in their time were attacked as costly, unmanageable, and unnecessary. And the ten case studies that follow are not unique. The stories of other beneficial government initiatives could have been told; for example, the development of radar, the eradication of polio, the commitment to land a man on the moon.

Yet it is also important to note that while the activist principle embodied in these case studies remains valid and instructive, some of the actions initiated by the government were flawed, morally complacent, or manipulated by the marketplace. Some decisions were guided by self-interest and the consequences were detrimental. For example, while we celebrate the ingenuity that built the Panama Canal and the transcontinental railroad, at the same time we must also recognize the arrogance that led America to enforce its will on a sovereign nation and ignore the cruel conditions and dangers that immigrant Chinese rail workers had to confront. The examples cited are bold endeavors, decisions made ͘y visionary leaders, but we must also recognize the flaws in some of these initiatives. The specifics too often are warnings, a reminder to put these achievements in perspective, and to apply moral standards to future national undertakings.

I AM NOT A historian, and this book is at its heart not a history. It is a narrative implicitly animated by the real-world experiences I had and the lessons I learned while working in a time of economic crisis with New York's Municipal Assistance Corporation (MAC) for eighteen years and during my tenure as an ambassador. Fundamentally, however, I have always been a banker, and this book is at its core a banker's call for action.

In opposition to the voices who choose to ignore the many successful examples from our nation's past (including those recounted in these pages) to argue that government intervention in the economy is always wasteful and ill-considered, this book is an appeal that we treat the renewal of our infrastructure as a necessary federal capital investment and not as just another expense item. In the epilogue I will offer a plan for establishing a National Infrastructure Bank. It is a program for creating an entity that will finance major infrastructure improvements with public, private, and international capital. This is a bank that will help America in a time of great economic crisis to finance public projects in a way similar to the European Investment Bank, which has underwritten high-speed rail networks. It will allow the country to keep pace with China where, starting in 2006, $200 billion will be invested in railways over four years.

Ultimately, this book offers a choice. Either we learn from our history and support a program that encourages the federal government to make significant investments to improve the way we live and work; or we complacently let time continue to take its toll on a great, yet aging nation. The past, the stories, and the leaders in this book remind us, need not be simply past. We as a nation must find the courage and the will to learn from our history, and then act.

The Louisiana Purchase

NAKED, DRIPPING RIVULETS OF water, bristling with an in-dignant fury, Napoléon Bonaparte rose from his bath. Red-faced, he shouted at his shocked brothers, Joseph and Lucien. "It is my idea. I conceived it, and I shall go through with it. . . . Do you understand?" he warned.

At that moment the brothers realized their protests had failed; Napoléon's mind was set. All they could do was listen with fear and deference while the naked First Consul of France upbraided them. As the tirade continued, an astonished valet collapsed to the floor in a faint. The two brothers did not even dare turn their heads to look.

Finally, his rage spent, Napoléon descended back into his tub.

Water splashed over the two brothers. Yet they stood without complaint in their wet clothes until at last Napoléon announced they were dismissed.

That incident in the bath at the Tuileries on April 7, 1803, set in motion historic events. Napoléon had reached a decision that would give him the funds to finance a war against England—if his plan to sell not just the port of New Orleans but the entire Louisiana Territory to the fledging United States of America succeeded. And it was a decision that would allow President Thomas Jefferson to double the size of the nation in a single stroke—if he could find the boldness to put aside his own concerns about the constitutional limitations on executive power, the resolve to stand up to congressional opposition, and the initiative to spend an unprecedented fortune of government funds to purchase foreign territory.

MORE THAN A CENTURY earlier, René-Robert Cavelier, Sieur de La Salle, had led a flotilla of canoes down the Mississippi River in search of "a port on the Gulf of Mexico on which could be formed a French settlement to serve as a base for conquests upon the Spaniards at the first outbreak of hostilities." When he finally reached the Gulf in 1682, a triumphant La Salle, citing the European "doctrine of discovery" of unoccupied lands, claimed for France all the territory drained by the Mississippi River from Canada to the Gulf of Mexico. La Salle named it Louisiana, in honor of King Louis XIV.

In 1718, a settlement was built on the strategic Gulf port La Salle had claimed. It was called Nouvelle Orléans, a tribute to

Philippe, duc d'Orléans and regent of France. By the time of the American Revolution, Nouvelle Orléans had become a busy commercial port, and the colonists recognized the importance of this settlement and the adjacent lands to their new country's future. The port of New Orleans controlled the navigation of the Mississippi River and was vital for the shipment of the colonies' agricultural products to Europe. And no less significant, the Louisiana Territory also loomed as the gateway to westward expansion.

Yet for decades New Orleans and the Louisiana Territory had been blithely traded back and forth between the European powers. In 1762, in the aftermath of the French and Indian War, France transferred New Orleans and the territory west of the Mississippi to Spain. The following year, the French territories east of the Mississippi, including Canada, were ceded to Britain. Then in 1784, Spain peremptorily closed the lower Mississippi and New Orleans to foreigners. Jefferson expressed the new nation's anger and concern: "There is on the globe one single spot, the possession of which is our natural and habitual enemy. It is New Orleans through which the produce of three-eighths of our territory must pass to market." But then eleven years later this dispute which had disrupted the young country's economy was resolved. In 1795, Spain signed Pinckney's Treaty with the United States, reopening New Orleans and restoring merchants' "right of deposit" to store goods in the port.

America rejoiced. But the country's commercial prosperity was soon threatened again. Worse, this time the nation's security was also in jeopardy. In 1799, Napoléon Bonaparte seized power in France.

• • •

NAPOLEON ASSUMED THE TITLE of First Consul at a time of troubled, increasingly tense relations between France and the United States. French privateers were routinely raiding American ships. An enraged Congress had passed a bill in 1798 empowering American warships to retaliate: all French privateers were fair game.

As a result, diplomatic relations between the two nations were severed. When an anxious President John Adams sent a delegation to France hoping to negotiate a peace treaty, a $250,000 bribe was demanded by French officials as payment for simply the right to open the discussions. Speaking for the indignant American delegation, John Marshall declared that his country would not even pay "a sixpence," and he returned home to a hero's welcome. As the nation cheered, Alexander Hamilton called for war. Hostilities, perhaps even an invasion of the United States, were, he insisted, a certainty. President Adams dismissed fears of an invasion, but nevertheless mobilized the army.

Then, on December 14, 1799, George Washington died. The country went into mourning for the singular man whose character and strength of purpose had guided the nation since its beginning. On the other side of the ocean, Napoléon orchestrated a grandiose memorial pageant for Washington, lauding his "moderation, disinterestedness, and wisdom."

Yet despite the dictator's praise for the man who symbolized republicanism, America was not lulled. The specter of Napoléon was a key issue in the bitterly contested presidential election of 1800. Federalists accused Thomas Jefferson, who had served for four years as the American minister at the court of Louis XVI, of being the "man of choice of France." Jefferson, in response, warned that his opponent, Alexander Hamilton, would become another dictator, an American Bonaparte.

Distancing himself from his old French allies, Jefferson won the election. The country's fears of Napoléon and his ambitions, however, were prescient. The dictator was determined to reestablish France's empire in the New World—and central to his plan was for the French flag to once again fly over the port of New Orleans and the Louisiana Territory.

Napoléon moved quickly, and on several fronts. He sent an army commanded by his brother-in-law Charles Leclerc to suppress a revolt by slaves and free blacks in France's richest colony, the Caribbean island of Saint-Domingue (now Haiti and the Dominican Republic). The island, Napoléon hoped, would serve as his primary naval base for his eventual assault of North America.

As his expeditionary force prepared to land in Saint-Domingue, Napoléon also employed diplomacy to realize his dream of a North American empire. He quietly negotiated in 1800 the Treaty of San Ildefonso with Spain. This treaty would return the Louisiana Territory to the French in exchange for France's commitment to install the Spanish king's son-in-law as king of Italy.

Although the deliberations had been conducted in great secrecy, the impending retrocession of the Louisiana Territory soon became known in Washington. President Jefferson had no doubt about what the prospect of a French New Orleans would mean to his country. He wrote that "this little event, of France possessing herself of Louisiana . . . is the embryo of a tornado which will burst on the countries on both sides of the Atlantic and involve in its effects their highest destinies." He was willing to go to war to prevent Louisiana's being taken over by the French.

Yet Jefferson also realized that a war with mighty France could prove disastrous to the new, still unsteady nation. "If we can settle happily the difficulties of the Mississippi," he fervently hoped, "I think we may promise ourselves smooth seas during our time."

Jefferson decided that as an alternative to war the United States should try to purchase the city of New Orleans and portions of the Louisiana Territory east of the Mississippi River, an area comprising the present-day southern portions of the states of Alabama and Mississippi, and most of Florida. He dispatched Robert Livingston as the American minister to France with the instructions to negotiate this deal.

"You have come to a very corrupt world," Napoléon warned Livingston when the American minister arrived in 1801. It was an assessment a despairing Livingston began to understand more fully after he started dealing with France's chief negotiator, Talleyrand, the foreign minister.

Exiled for two years in the United States during the French Revolution, Talleyrand despised America and the Americans. He had no inclination to see the negotiations move forward. Adding to Livingston's consternation, Talleyrand demanded, as was his customary practice, a bribe before there could be any serious discussions.

Assisting Talleyrand in the negotiations was the Treasury minister, François de Barbé-Marbois, and a young diplomat in the Foreign Ministry, Louis-André Pichon. Barbé-Marbois was a man of great integrity and Livingston felt that with him there was at least the prospect of meaningful negotiations. But Pichon ultimately proved more valuable. The Americans began channeling disinformation through him. Jefferson, working with Secretary of State James Madison, convinced the French diplomat, for example, that the United States would sign a treaty with England if the negotiations failed. Pichon believed this, and passed the intelligence on to his superiors. As Livingston's efforts continued to flounder, a disappointed Jefferson resorted more and more to relying on the Pichon channel to spread false reports. In time, Livingston's dispatches to the president and the secretary of state were simply ignored.

America was frustrated, but the talks between the two nations continued. Without warning, however, the situation suddenly turned ominous. As France waited to assume control of the Louisiana Territory, in 1802 the Spanish agent in New Orleans, acting on orders from King Charles IV of Spain, revoked America's access to the port's warehouses.

The Federalist Party called for war. There was talk in Kentucky and the western territories of secession and acting on their own to seize control of the lower Mississippi and the prize of New Orleans. Even Jefferson grew despondent. War with France over Louisiana, he decided, was inevitable.

One influential presidential adviser, though, counseled restraint. Pierre-Samuel DuPont de Nemours was a native of France who had worked with Jefferson to negotiate the Treaty of Paris ending the American Revolution. He went on to serve as president of the French National Assembly, but when his pleas for moderate reform proved unpopular, DuPont and his son Victor emigrated to America. Now the DuPonts were advising Jefferson during the Louisiana crisis.

The cost of waging a war for New Orleans, Pierre DuPont insisted, was likely to be greater than the cost of buying the city. He urged the president to continue the negotiations. Jefferson, although not sanguine, agreed it was worth one last attempt.

The president decided to send James Monroe, who had served as President Washington's minister to France before representing Virginia in Congress and becoming the state's governor, to Paris as minister extraordinary. "All eyes, all hopes, are now fixed on you," the president wrote his old friend before Monroe sailed to France. "For on the event of this mission depend the future destinies of this republic."

Monroe was authorized to spend $9,375,000 for the purchase of New Orleans and West Florida. If this bid was unsuccessful, he was to try to purchase just New Orleans, or, at the very least, gain the right of access to the port and the Mississippi. An additional $2 million was allocated by Congress for "expenses"—a tacit acknowledgment of the cost of doing business with Talleyrand.

Robert Livingston took the appointment of the new American minister as a personal affront. He fumed while he waited for Monroe to arrive. He was certain that no emissary could change the meandering course of the negotiations, or the prospects for success. "There never was government," he wrote bitterly to Madison, "in which less could be done by negotiation than here."

But Livingston was wrong. France's unwillingness to make a deal was about to change. Swarms of mosquitoes, as fate would ironically have it, would determine large and historic events.

• • •

THE ARMY NAPOLÉON HAD sent to Saint-Domingue had moved swiftly and effectively to crush the rebellion. Toussaint L'Ouverture, the leader of the rebel forces, had been captured and sent to a French prison. It seemed only a matter of time before the last pockets of resistance were overcome and French control of the sugar-rich island was completely restored. But then swarms of infected mosquitoes attacked the French force and yellow fever spread through the helpless ranks. More than 24,000 French soldiers died. In November 1802, the disease claimed Leclerc, and the already debilitated force, now without its commander, fell into disarray. Napoléon conceded he might never regain control of the island. "Damn sugar, damn coffee, damn colonies," he fumed.

At the same time as he was losing control to the rebels of this crucial base for a Louisiana invasion, Napoléon's attention was diverted by another adversary closer to home. A war with Britain suddenly loomed.

To prepare for the transport of his army to North America, Napoléon had ordered that the French fleet be increased. When George III received reports of this new naval construction, he reviewed the intelligence, and decided the French were preparing to attack England. The alarmed monarch, as he explained, "judged it expedient to adopt additional measures of precaution." Britain reneged on its promise to evacuate Malta and instead prepared for another war with France.

With the likelihood of war with Britain, with Saint-Domingue lost, Napoléon, always practical, always decisive, realized his dream for an empire in America could not be sustained. France had neither the troops nor the money to occupy the entire Mississippi Valley and also fight a European war. There was, however, a way he could extricate France from North America and in the process raise the funds necessary to finance a war with Britain. He would sell not just New Orleans but the entire Louisiana Territory to the United States.

When Napoléon's brothers Joseph and Lucien heard rumors of this plan, they rushed to the Tuileries to try to dissuade him. They believed that if Louisiana were not sold, a war with Britain would be averted. Joseph, however, had an additional motivation: the British had promised to pay him £100,000 if he could convince his brother not to sell the territory.

But the tense confrontation in the bath at the Tuileries between the three brothers only served to reinforce Napoléon's resolve. The First Consul was adamant. His mind was now set. He would try to sell the entire Louisiana Territory.

FOUR DAYS AFTER, ON April 11, 1803, Talleyrand approached Livingston and very casually asked if, perhaps, the United States was interested in acquiring "the whole of Louisiana." Livingston thought the foreign minister was toying with him. After all, there had been, he would write, "many deceptions that had been previously practiced upon him." Besides, Monroe was still en route to Paris. It made no practical sense for the negotiations suddenly to escalate before the new emissary's arrival.

Yet Livingston could not help but wonder: Was Talleyrand serious? He had no instructions beyond the acquisition of New Orleans and the Floridas. In fact, he had not even considered the possibility of such a monumental purchase. Nevertheless, Livingston decided to play along. He offered 20 million francs.

Too low, Talleyrand countered. But think about it, the foreign minister advised.

Livingston doubted that the matter would ever again be discussed. Just days later, though, at a dinner party celebrating Monroe's arrival, Barbé-Marbois raised the possibility of France's selling "not only New Orleans, but the whole colony without reservation." Livingston was stunned. It was true! After all the years of tedious, meandering discussions, a deal—a colossal deal—was finally a possibility. His country had the opportunity not simply to purchase New Orleans but the entire territory. America would control the Mississippi River and its western tributaries out to the Rocky Mountains.

An elated Livingston and Monroe quickly entered into serious negotiations. Napoléon had instructed Barbé-Marbois to receive a minimum price of 50 million francs. "For less than that sum I will not treat," Napoléon insisted. The finance minister, however, believed the First Consul was setting the price too low. He informed the Americans Napoléon would accept 100 million francs, and nothing less. There was also, he explained, an indemnity that had to be paid against claims by American merchants for cargoes captured at sea by French warships.

The finance minister was demanding a fortune, but the American negotiators were not deterred. They were confident the price could be "reduced to reasonable limits." An excited Livingston wrote to Madison to inform the secretary of state that they would "do all we can to cheapen the purchase, but my present sentiment is that we shall buy."

With both sides eager for a deal, the discussions moved forward very rapidly. On April 15, Monroe and Livingston offered 50 million francs. Barbé-Marbois listened without comment, but days later returned to the table and announced that Napoléon had responded "very coldly."

On April 29, the Americans gamely presented a new offer. The United States would pay 50 million francs for Louisiana and an additional 20 million francs as credit against the debts owed by the French to the American merchants. The finance minister disingenuously countered that Napoléon would not accept less than 60 million for the territory. Without consulting their government, Livingston and Monroe agreed. The United States would pay 80 million francs, a total of $15 million: 60 million francs ($11,250,000) for all the land and an additional 20 million francs ($3,750,000) for the indemnity.

The specific boundaries of the land involved in the purchase were still vague. But now that the price had been established, Talleyrand coolly conceded that France would not bother with too many of the other details. "You have made a noble bargain for yourselves," he told Monroe and Livingston, "and I suppose you will make the most of it." The final agreement, though, made it clear that French and Spanish ships would pay the same port duties in New Orleans as American vessels. Additionally, all citizens of Louisiana would have the same universal rights as those granted to other Americans under the Constitution.

On May 2, 1803, the treaty was signed by Barbé-Marbois and Livingston and Monroe. "We have lived long, but this is the noblest work of our whole lives," Livingston rejoiced. "The treaty . . .

has not been obtained by force. From this day the United States take their place among the powers of the first rank."

ONLY NOW THE COUNTRY needed to find the funds to close the deal. "America had bought Louisiana for a song," Jefferson celebrated when he heard the news on July 3. But it was still a very costly "song." The price not only exceeded the American negotiators' congressional authority by almost $6 million, it also was a sum the United States could not seem to afford. The nation's total revenues in the previous year were about $10 million—$5 million less than the French had been promised.

America tried to persuade Napoléon to take government bonds as financing, but the French refused to accept this arrangement. War with Britain was imminent; funds were needed right away. A further impediment: the long-term credit of the American government was, in the estimation of French bankers, an untested and perhaps unreliable proposition. It was a gamble French banks were unprepared to accept.

Desperate, Monroe and Livingston began to search for alternative financing. They knocked on bankers' doors all over Europe without success. Finally, they persuaded Baring Brothers, a British bank, and Hope & Co., a Dutch financial institution, to pay the French government $15 million immediately in cash. In return, the two financial houses would receive U.S. government bonds that would repay the entire sum at 6 percent over the course of fifteen years. The total cost to the government would, therefore, be approximately $27 million. The money was now in place.

Yet there were still other significant problems to be resolved before the treaty could be ratified. New England Federalists in Congress worried that they would lose the influence that they had enjoyed since the founding of the republic. With the new territory, the nation's commercial base would shift to the South or the West, and the power of the eastern families, they feared, would be diminished.

Others argued that the terms of the deal were expensive and the specific boundaries imprecise. "We are to give money of which we have too little for land of which we have already too much," wrote Fisher Ames, an influential Massachusetts congressman, articulating a widely held sentiment.

Even Jefferson had some misgivings. He had been a strong supporter of states' rights and he worried that the Constitution did not contain any specific provisions empowering the federal government to purchase land. He gave serious thought to proposing a constitutional amendment before the deal could proceed.

But Jefferson soon put aside his misgivings. The opportunity, he reasoned, offered much for the nation. "While the property and sovereignty of the Mississippi and its waters secure an independent outlet for the produce of the western states," he acknowledged, before going on to add with a visionary prescience, "the fertility of the country, its climate and extent, promise in the season important aids to our treasury, an ample provision for our posterity, and a wide-spread field for the blessings of freedom." He would act boldly and decisively. The treaty, the president urged, must be approved.

On October 20, 1803, the Senate ratified the treaty by a vote of 24 to 7. Spain declared that the Treaty of San Ildefonso prohibited

France from selling Louisiana to a rival nation, but it lacked the military power to block the sale. On November 30, Spain formally returned Louisiana to France. A month later, on December 30, 1803, the Stars and Stripes was raised for the first time over the port of New Orleans.

WHAT A DEAL JEFFERSON had engineered! He had not received permission from Congress to acquire any territory other than the city of New Orleans and parts of Florida. He had no authority to pay a sum in excess of $9 million. He had no clear knowledge of the boundaries of his acquisition. He had genuine doubts about the constitutionality of his purchase. Yet Jefferson had found the political courage and the initiative to use federal funds to make an unprecedented investment.

The returns were immediate. The size of the nation was immediately doubled—828,000 square miles purchased at the cost of about four cents an acre. War had been averted. The Mississippi was secured for trade.

But the long-term rewards were even more spectacular. The total price, with interest, of $27 million was enormous. These bonds, however, confirmed the credit of the United States in the international financial markets. Their orderly repayment during the subsequent fifteen years established America's place as a world power, a responsible nation with the potential for even greater growth.

Further, the addition of such a vast tract of land to the original colonies helped to democratize America. One of the first decisions made by Jefferson after the treaty was signed was to send two of his close associates, Meriwether Lewis and William Clark, to map and explore the previously uncharted wilderness. They provided the government with the first specific information about the majestic, bountiful land the nation had purchased. And with the country's expansion there were now new and ample opportunities for its citizens to become property owners. One hundred and sixty–acre tracts were carved out of the Louisiana Territory and sold by the government for $1.64 an acre. The long process of building America into a more open, egalitarian, and capitalist society moved forward.

Yet, most important, it was this courageous investment of federal funds, an act that was without precedent and strongly opposed, that not only transformed the country and its people but also ensured the republic's future. With the Louisiana Purchase, America's political destiny to become a unique and powerful nation stretching across the continent from sea to shining sea was confirmed. A magnificent future was within the republic's grasp.

The Erie Canal

STANDING ON THE BANKS of the Mohawk River, Cadwallader Colden watched with fascination as the snaking line of birch-bark canoes made their swift way upstream toward Oneida Lake. As the Indians rhythmically plunged their paddles into the water on that afternoon in 1724, an idea began to take shape in the scientist's mind.

Colden, educated at Edinburgh University, had come to America from his native Ireland at the request of the governor of New York Province to do a geographical survey of western New York and at the same time report on relations between the French colonialists and the local Indian tribes. As he journeyed across the rugged country and observed, Colden was struck by the ingenuity the Indians used to deliver their furs to the French. Setting out from Albany, they'd carry their goods a short 16 miles overland to Schenectady and the Mohawk River; then they'd paddle their canoes upriver to Oneida Lake; until they'd finally drift, as he wrote, "with the current down the Onondoga [now the Ostwego] River to Lake Ontario." The Indians, Colden realized with admiration, had devised an easily navigable, calm water route through the Appalachian Mountains. And this shortcut sparked his thoughts.

Why not, he decided in a burst of inspiration, create a trail of waterways from the industries of the eastern seaboard to the rich wilderness of the Northwest territories? Why not connect the Great Lakes to the Atlantic Ocean by a path of integrated rivers? Such a water route, he began to see with increasing clarity, would be a quick and economical highway that would carry people and trade back and forth between the eastern colonies and the natural bounty in the New World's frontier. It would be, he felt certain, the path that would encourage the colonies to spread westward.

It was not until nearly one hundred years later, in 1817, when the first trenches for this interconnecting waterway were dug, that Colden's practical vision would begin to be transformed into a reality. And after the 363-mile Erie Canal was completed eight years later, this swift path from the Hudson River to Lake Erie, a route that, as the inaugural proclamation announced, "wedded the waters" between the Great Lakes and the Atlantic Ocean, would have consequences far beyond Colden's original expectations. Not only did this waterway open the western frontier, but it was crucial to New York City's becoming the nation's chief port and one of the world's great metropolitan centers.

The canal was a state-funded engineering marvel that demonstrated, as the eighty-year-old former president Thomas Jefferson observed, "the capability of nations to execute great enterprises." The success of the Erie Canal helped further establish the precedent that a visionary and innovative government can finance and build significant projects that will dramatically improve the nation's wealth and quality of life.

Yet the creation of the Erie Canal is also a history of tenacity, a century-long tale of perseverance by far-seeing, resolute, inventive, and often stubborn individuals. It is the story of leaders who were inspired by the originality of Colden's insight; and who, with this possibility firmly rooted in their imagination, refused to surrender to any of the obstacles that either a shortsighted Politics or a malicious Nature put in the way of what they believed was in the best interests of the nation.

GEORGE WASHINGTON WAS WORRIED. Although he was no longer president, he had not abandoned his concern for the nation he had helped create. Out of office, in retirement, he grew anxious about the country's future.

For the United States to survive and prosper, the former president believed the country would need to develop its western territories. No less troubling, he feared that if America did not firmly establish its ties to the settlers in these frontier lands, then European powers would colonize the West. The opportunity to expand the country across the continent would be lost.

It was essential that government begin "applying the cement of interest," Washington insisted in a 1785 letter to Patrick Henry, the governor of Virginia, "to bind all parts of the Union together by indispensable bonds—especially of binding that part of it which lies immediately west of us, to the middle States." And a canal, Washington believed with passion, would be "the cement" that would firmly and indispensably bond the western lands to the rest of America.

With President Jefferson's encouragement, Washington formed the Patowmack Company to build a canal along the Potomac River (as it is now known). It would run from Alexandria, Virginia, and continue westward through the mountains beyond the nation's capital.

It was an inspired idea, and it had influential and well-known supporters. Nevertheless, the project was immediately besieged by managerial, labor, and financial problems. When Washington died in 1799, an already troubled company began to unravel. Still, the Patowmack Company managed to flounder on until, at last, it went bankrupt in 1810.

Yet despite all its problems and its ultimate failure, the Patowmack Company had succeeded in popularizing the former president's original vision: A canal tying the East to the western territories was vital to the new republic's future.

AS THE IDEA OF a Potomac canal began to attract supporters in Virginia, Christopher Colles, an Irish immigrant to America, tried to apply his practical experience to the building of an interconnecting waterway based in New York. In Ireland, Colles had worked on improving navigation on the Shannon River; now he hoped to use this expertise to benefit his new homeland.

While Washington was busy trying to attract investors to his

Patowmack Company, Colles went off to make an impressively detailed survey of New York's waterways. When he was finished, Colles presented his findings to the New York state legislature; unlike the former president, he believed that government, not private individuals, should finance the construction of a system that would play such an integral part in the further development of the new nation.

The paper that Colles presented to the legislature in 1784 was entitled "Proposals for the Speedy Settlement of the Vast and Unappropriated Lands of the Western Frontiers of New York, and for the Improvement of the Inland Navigation Between Albany and Oswego." Although its title was long-winded, Colles's paper was a succinct, well-reasoned call for practical action. It emphasized the advantages of travel on the calm Mohawk River waters, and detailed the economic benefits that would result from a canal that connected the nation's seacoast to its interior. Insightfully, Colles bolstered his argument by pointing out the military advantages in such a canal. "In times of war," he wrote, "provisions and military stores may be moved with facility in sufficient quantity to answer any emergency."

The legislature listened attentively to Colles's presentation, but in the end refused to allocate funds. Still, his carefully presented ideas got the citizens and politicians of New York State thinking. Perhaps, they began increasingly to reflect, a canal *did* make sense.

NEW YORK STATE SENATOR Philip Schuyler had been particularly intrigued by Colles's argument for a canal. More important, he was an influential voice in the legislature. A scion of New York's Dutch aristocracy and father-in-law of Alexander Hamilton, Schuyler had served in the Provincial Army in the 1750s and then went on to become a fabled Continental Army general during the Revolution. After independence, he was elected to the New York State Senate.

It was in 1791 when he was a state senator that Schuyler was approached by Elkanah Watson. Watson, part adventurer, part entrepreneur, had returned to the United States after running a business in France. Upon his arrival in Virginia, Watson had a chance encounter with former president George Washington. Washington talked enthusiastically to the young man about his plan for a Potomac River Canal. It was this small conversation, Watson would later say, that first kindled "a canal flame in my mind."

Six years later, Watson, now living in Albany, New York, and helping to organize a local bank, led an expedition to explore the possibility of building a canal that would connect the Hudson River to Lake Erie. Once his report on the trip was completed, the affable Watson, a man with a unique ability to align himself with celebrated mentors, presented it to Schuyler.

Schuyler, whose interest in a canal had first been prodded years earlier by Colles, read Watson's paper with a growing enthusiasm. By the time he was finished, Schuyler was convinced that Watson's plan for two canals—one from the Hudson to Lake Ontario, the other from the Hudson to Lake Champlain—was both inspired and practical. He was determined to help. Schuyler used his considerable influence to convince the state senate to finance two enterprises—the Western Inland Lock Navigation

Company and the Northern Inland Lock Navigation Company—that together would construct the two canals.

The canals were never built. And in time, the companies quietly went out of business. Nevertheless, the collaboration between Schuyler and Watson had established a principle that would prove significant: New York State was willing to finance a canal.

AFTER THE DISMAL FAILURES of the two lock navigation companies, the public and political support for a New York canal seemed to disappear. For over a decade the project was largely ignored, and further political efforts were abandoned. But then, in 1807, it was suddenly revitalized. From the depths of debtors' prison, a voice reached out and once again captured people's imagination and ignited their enthusiasm.

Jesse Hawley was a western New York flour merchant whose business had collapsed because of his inability to make timely shipments to his customers. Both the rough upstate roads and the choppy Mohawk River had proved to be unmanageable routes; his flour rarely reached its destinations. When the overextended Hawley could not pay his bills, he was sentenced to twenty months in debtors' prison.

He used the time in jail to mull over his failure, and to write. Under the pseudonym of "Hercules," Hawley published a series of essays in the Genesee, New York, *Messenger*. These essays offered a logical and persuasively articulated plan that would solve the problems of transporting goods across the state. He urged the building of a canal to link the city of Buffalo, on the eastern end of

Lake Erie, to the city of Utica in central New York State, via the Mohawk River, the Hudson's largest tributary.

"The trade of almost all the lakes in North America," Hawley predicted with confidence, ". . . would center at New York," and "in a century [that] island would be covered with buildings and population of its city." With impressive prescience, Hawley, the untrained amateur, accurately specified the route that a canal should (and two decades later would) follow. And he cannily estimated that it would cost $6 million; the actual expense was $7 million.

At the time, though, the great accomplishment of these essays was that they helped once again to create support for a canal in the state legislature. In 1808, two New York assemblymen, Joshua Forman and Benjamin Wright (who himself had drawn maps of the Mohawk River for the ill-fated Western Inland Lock Navigation Company), proposed a bill that would allocate $600 to survey canal routes.

The bill passed, and James Geddes, a surveyor, was hired by the state. Geddes threw himself into the task. He charted, he would write, "the rivers, streams and waters . . . in the usual route of communication between the Hudson River and Lake Erie." When he was done, he announced that a canal was indeed feasible. He did, however, warn that it would be a massive undertaking. Planning, labor, and costs would be considerable challenges. He conceded that unfortunately he was "born very many years too soon" to ever see it completed.

Despite these caveats, Joshua Forman, one of the original sponsors of the bill that had led to Geddes's commission, was encouraged. The survey, he felt, had proved the project "practicable beyond [the] most sanguine expectations." He went to President Thomas Jefferson to request federal support for the canal.

Jefferson listened; and then declared that the New York project was "little more than madness." It was, the president thundered, much too ambitious, an idea that was a hundred years ahead of its time.

Forman was undeterred. "The state of New York," the defiant assemblyman informed the president, "would never rest until [the canal] was accomplished."

But while the efforts continued to raise canal financing elsewhere, they had little tangible results. By 1810, Thomas Eddy, a director of the struggling Western Company, and Jonas Platt, a New York state senator, had come to believe in fact that a private company could never succeed in building a canal. The two men decided that government would need to control the project, and they formulated a plan for a New York State Canal Commission. For the commission to be effective, they realized it would need to be bipartisan. And so, in what would prove to be an inspired gesture, they reached out to DeWitt Clinton.

DEWITT CLINTON WAS A popular and influential Republican politician. He had resigned from the U.S. Senate in 1803 to run for mayor of New York. He was elected for three terms, and also served simultaneously from 1806 to 1811 in the State Senate, and then from 1811 to 1813 as lieutenant governor.

The "Hercules" essays had convinced Clinton of "the practicability of such a canal," and now he readily agreed to support a Canal Commission. With his vocal backing, the commission was ratified by the state assembly and $3,000 was appropriated for its expenses.

In recognition of his efforts (and his influence), Clinton was appointed to the Canal Commission, along with fellow Republicans Simon DeWitt (Clinton's cousin and the state surveyor) and Peter Porter. The Federalist members were Gouverneur Morris, Stephen van Rensselaer, William North, and Thomas Eddy.

It was a truly bipartisan group, and, as history would demonstrate, a visionary one. The New York commissioners put aside their many differences to form a united group that, despite all political obstacles, would persevere to lead one of the great engineering achievements of all time.

WITH THE SHARED SENSE that they were embarking on a great mission, the Canal Commission members began their work. Using Geddes's survey and the "Hercules" essays as their guides, in the summer of 1810 the new state commissioners set out to explore possible canal routes. It was a rough trip.

DeWitt Clinton's journal vividly describes the distinguished statesmen's discomforting journey along the Mohawk River wilderness. Day after day, they battled "an army of bed bugs, aided by a light infantry in the shape of fleas, and a regiment of mosquito cavalry." The locals, too, did not welcome them; one farmer, apparently enraged by the spectacle of the august commissioners' arrival on his property, responded by hurling a pitchfork at them.

But the commissioners continued on, and in March 1811, they submitted their findings to the legislature. It created a furor.

Matter-of-factly, the commission dismissed all previous suggestions about merely improving river navigation. Instead, it proposed a full-scale canal.

The Lake Ontario route, however, was categorically rejected. The commissioners criticized its limited supply of water, its impracticality for schooners and larger boats, and the large number of transshipments that would be required for a trip from the seacoast to Lake Ontario.

The Lake Erie route had none of these disadvantages. There was plentiful water; this would make building a canal easier since it could be constructed on an inclined plane and fed from the lock. And the resulting absence of locks on most sections of the canal would greatly reduce maintenance fees. The Erie route, the report declared, made the most practical and economic sense.

The canal, the commission predicted, would be a good investment. It would make money, and it would facilitate commerce throughout the state. Nevertheless, the report resolutely concluded that the canal should not be financed or run by the private sector. "Too great a national interest is at stake. It must not become the subject of a job, or a fund for speculation. . . . Such large expenditures can be more economically made under public authority, than by the care and vigilance of any company."

The New York state legislature agreed: The canal should be a public enterprise. In April 1811, it authorized the Canal Commission to seek funding from the federal government and from other states.

GOUVERNEUR MORRIS AND DEWITT Clinton, as representatives of the commission, went to Washington, D.C., determined to reverse the results of the unsuccessful appeal that had been made years earlier to President Jefferson. In preparation for their meeting with President James Madison they had prepared a memo that, they felt, persuasively enumerated the many benefits of the canal. It would "encourage agriculture, promote commerce and manufacturers, facilitate a free and general intercourse between different parts of the United States, tend to the aggrandizement and prosperity of the country, and consolidate and strengthen the Union."

Full of optimism, convinced of the rightness of their argument, Morris and Clinton confidently made their case. The president listened with apparent concentration. He nodded his head enthusiastically, as if mutely agreeing with every point they made.

When the presentation was concluded, Madison began by praising the commission's efforts. He then went on to share that he was "an enthusiast as to the advantages of interior navigation, by means of canals." But finally Madison said he could not offer federal support. It would be, he explained, unconstitutional. He conceded that he was "embarrassed by scruples deriving from his interpretation of the Constitution." Nevertheless, this was, he apologized with terse authority, the end of the discussion.

Morris and Clinton were discouraged, but they would not give up. They approached Albert Gallatin, secretary of the Treasury, who was a well-known advocate for transportation development. But Gallatin, too, was unsupportive; the impending war with Britain, he explained, restricted the availability of funds. Perhaps, the desperate commissioners countered, the Treasury could offer support in the form of land grants. Again, Gallatin refused.

So, the two commissioners began to approach the states adja-

cent to New York for funding. This time the response was not simply negative but entirely skeptical. "A railroad from the earth to
the moon could not be treated with more derision," an exasperated Clinton complained.

Despite the failure to raise financing, the commissioners did
not abandon their efforts. They simply chose another strategy:
New York State would need to build and finance the Erie Canal on
its own.

HOPING TO ATTRACT SUPPORTERS in the legislature, the Canal
Commission in March 1812 issued a new report. It was a shrewdly
practical document, insisting that the canal would be a money-
making investment for the state.

The report opened with a candid admission. The canal would
require more locks than had initially been planned and therefore
it would cost more than previously estimated: $6 million. But the
report breezily put this sum into perspective: "It is almost a con-
tradiction in terms to suppose that an expenditure of five or six
million, in ten or twenty years, can be a serious consideration to a
million men, enjoying one of the richest soils and finest climates
under heaven."

The report then went on to focus more solidly on the economics of building and financing a canal. A $5 million loan, the com-
missioners asserted, could be readily obtained from European
sources for a term of ten or fifteen years and at a rate of only
six percent.

According to the report's calculations, servicing this loan would
not be a problem. Within only twenty years, the legislators were as-

sured, the canal would carry an impressive 250,000 tons of freight annually. At a toll of $2.50 per ton, this, combined with other fees, would generate $1,250,000 each year. These proceeds, the commissioners stated, would not only be sufficient to pay the interest on the loan but also would bring a substantial profit to the state.

The report concluded by urging the state to take immediate action. "Things which twenty years ago a man would have been laughed at for believing, we now see," the commissioners reminded their fellow elected officials. However complicated the engineering challenges, however daunting the cost, the canal was a similar enterprise: a futuristic idea that could be made into a reality.

But while the report was bursting with a gung-ho confidence, sentiments ran similarly high among the canal's opponents. The project was dismissed as frivolous and as a drain on the nation's budget. "It would require the revenue of all the kingdoms of the earth, and the population of China, to accomplish it," mocked one state legislator.

To the Federalists, Clinton's motives were also suspect. His visit to Washington to meet with President Madison, they charged, had been "undertaken by him for electioneering purposes." Senator James A. Bayard railed that the intent was more "to open a road to the presidency than a canal from the lakes."

Gouverneur Morris acidly shot back at the commission's critics. The commissioners, he said, "must, nevertheless, have the hardihood to brave the sneers and sarcasm of men who, with too much pride to study, too much wit to think, undervalue what they do not understand, and condemn what they do not comprehend."

In the end, the canal supporters prevailed. On June 19, 1812, the legislature by a small majority ratified the report's findings. And in an accompanying bill, the commissioners were authorized to borrow a maximum of $5 million on the credit of the state and to sell the rights of the Western Inland Lock Navigation Company to raise additional funding.

THE COMMISSION'S CELEBRATION WAS short-lived. On the same day that New York ratified its plan to build the canal, President Madison declared war on Great Britain.

The commissioners tried at first to convince themselves that the War of 1812 would not impede the construction of the canal. In fact, war could very well make the project a priority; after all, there were military advantages in having a swift waterway route to the west.

But this logic proved to be only wishful thinking. With the outbreak of war, a flurry of large problems quickly followed. First, the hydrological and geographical surveys of the proposed canal route were suspended because of "military operations which are not favorable to internal improvements." Then, the English engineer chosen by the commission to oversee the project was prohibited from coming to New York; and the available American engineers were, it was conceded, too inexperienced. And finally, the hostilities made it impossible for the state to secure a European loan; no bank would lend a fortune to a nation whose future was in doubt.

Domestic political problems further undermined the project. DeWitt Clinton, the canal's most vocal advocate, was defeated in the 1812 presidential election, and the loss left his reputation tarnished and his influence diminished. At the same time, the Federalist Party, whose members nearly uniformly supported the project, was in shambles. With the party's opposition to both Madison and the war, it no longer had the power to rally the legislature.

In 1814, the New York state legislature canceled the commission's right to borrow capital on behalf of the state. The commissioners were devastated. They had, one observer commiserated, "given up all hopes of the legislature being induced again to take up the subject, or to adopt any measure to prosecute the scheme."

Clinton, too, acknowledged the totality of his defeat. "Without power and without money," he wrote, the canal was an impossibility. This was, he accepted with a grim certitude, the end of his dream.

YET ONCE THE WAR of 1812 was concluded, the nation looked back at the hostilities; and now from the perspective of experience, the strategic and economic necessity of a canal became increasingly apparent. Much of the war, for example, had been fought in the west. With its skill at inland navigation, Britain had been able to dispatch forces and supplies westward. But the United States had struggled to transport men, weapons, and provisions to this front—and these failures had lost battles.

Additionally, the cost of supplying the troops in the western territories had been crippling. An 1816 report by General James Tallmadge, who had commanded the wartime forces in upstate New York, offered daunting testimony: the cost of shipping a single barrel of pork inland to feed the troops was $126; a single cannon, fabricated back east for $400, wound up costing an additional $2,000 by the time it was delivered to the troops on the shores of Lake Erie.

The war had also shown the need to end the nation's reliance on imports and foreign manufacturers. In the future, America would need to be more economically self-reliant. And one way to accomplish this, it was generally agreed, would be to reap the natural benefits of the continent's vast interior wilderness. But first there needed to be a practical way to transport goods out west, and natural resources back east. A canal, people were once again beginning to realize, was vital if the country was to remain militarily strong and economically independent.

With the end of the war, though, the possibility of a Lake Ontario route for the canal was uniformly dismissed. Relations between Canada and the United States had soured; the war had left the country suspicious about its northern neighbor's secret alliances and hidden intentions. All the discussions now centered on the Lake Erie route.

But even as sentiment for a canal was once again building, its longtime public champion was too preoccupied to offer his support. DeWitt Clinton was busy trying to save his own future. His political career was in near ruin.

New York's Tammany organization, Clinton's bitter enemies, had finally succeeded in undermining his support in the Democratic Party. They had persuaded Governor Daniel Tompkins to remove Clinton from his position as mayor of New York.

Dismissed from the mayoralty, Clinton's political life was apparently over. Yet the ambitious and tenacious Clinton would, against all odds, manage to save his career. And in the process, he would ensure that the long-doomed Erie Canal would be built, too.

OUT OF POWER, HIS political capital spent, Clinton nevertheless decided to make a new push for the canal. This time, by necessity, he devised a different approach. He would not try to sell the project to the state legislators. Instead, he would appeal directly to the people.

On December 3, 1815, Clinton, along with fellow commissioners Eddy and Platt, convened a meeting of distinguished New Yorkers. The purpose was to persuade these influential citizens of the necessity of a canal. Before the session ended, they too agreed that the time had come to reach out to the citizens of New York. It was decided that Clinton would draft a statement outlining the argument for a canal; and then this document would be circulated as a petition around the state.

Clinton's thirteen-page manifesto was inspired.

It was grounded in history: "The prosperity of ancient Egypt and China may in a great degree be attributed to their inland navigation."

It looked to the future: The canal would make New York City "the great depot and warehouse of the western world . . . the greatest commercial city in the world."

It was pragmatic: The canal would cost $6 million, but the state could secure a loan for ten to fifteen years, and profits would certainly offset interest payments. Moreover, private landowners were willing to donate more than 100,000 acres of land, tracts worth more than $1 million.

It was impassioned: "Our merchants should not be robbed of their legitimate profits . . . public revenues should not be seriously impaired by dishonest smuggling, and . . . the commerce of our cities should not be supplanted by mercantile establishments of foreign countries."

It was poetic:

The whole line of canal will exhibit boats loaded with flour, pork, beef, pot and pearl ashes, flaxseed, wheat, barley, corn, hemp, wool, flax, iron, lead, copper, salt, gypsum, coal, tar, fur, peltry, ginseng, bees-wax, cheese, butter, lard, staves, lumber and the other valuable productions of our country; and also with merchandise from all parts of the world. Great manufacturing establishments will spring up; agriculture will establish its granaries, and commerce its warehouses in all directions. Villages, towns, and cities will line the banks of the canal, and the shores of the Hudson from Erie to New York. The wilderness and the solitary place will become glad, and desert will rejoice and blossom as the rose.

And, above all, it was a mandate for action: "It is your incumbent duty to open, facilitate, and improve internal navigation . . . to create a new era in history, and to erect a work more stupendous, more magnificent, and more beneficial than has hereto been achieved by the human race."

Not surprising, the document enraged Clinton's opponents. The Martling Men, a group of New York City Republicans led by Martin Van Buren, were particularly vocal. They did not want Clinton to lead a historic undertaking, especially one that if it succeeded would no doubt restore his political career. Governor Tompkins argued that improved roads were preferable to the certain folly of "Clinton's canal."

But the response from citizens throughout the state was enthusiastic. The Canal Commission had organized meetings in the cities and towns along the path of the proposed canal and Clinton's manifesto was read out loud. More than 100,000 signatures were collected urging the legislature to fund construction of the Erie Canal.

The state assembly bowed to the unprecedented public pressure. In 1816, the assembly passed a bill authorizing a $2 million loan for both construction of the middle section of the Erie Canal, from the city of Rome to the Seneca River, and the Champlain Canal, a sixty-four-mile route from Watervliet on the Hudson to Lake Champlain.

BEFORE CLINTON AND HIS fellow commissioners could celebrate their victory, the state senate annulled the lower house's authorization. At Martin Van Buren's urging, the senators passed a motion stipulating that more extensive surveys needed to be completed and the exact route determined before the actual construction of the two canals could begin. The senators appropriated a trifling $20,000 to conduct these surveys.

Yet the commissioners refused to be defeated. Rather than complain about the meager sum allotted for such a monumental task, they decided to make the most of the funds they were given. They hired a surveyor to oversee the project. But this time they did not choose an expensive Englishman who, as one contemporary pointed out, "knows very little about the management and conducting of business in this country." Instead, they hired, for a lesser salary, an American.

A new, accurately detailed survey was quickly begun. After its completion in February 1817, the commission presented an exhaustive 174-page report to the state legislature. The bottom line, though, was succinct: The 353-mile project would cost $4.9 million, about $13,400 per mile.

The legislators in the assembly immediately wanted to know where this money, a breathtaking sum in 1817 dollars, would come from. Many of the assemblymen felt New York City should be taxed to pay for a substantial portion of the construction. As Elisha Williams, an assemblyman from Columbia County, argued: "Will not all the productions of this vast and fertile territory go to New York? . . . If this canal is to be a shower of gold, it will fall upon New York. . . . Are we to give her the means of enriching herself beyond all former example, and of monopolizing the trade of the whole world, and she pays nothing in return?"

The delegation from New York City, however, fervently objected to any special taxes. They pointed out that there would be cheap merchandise coming in from the west that would discourage people from buying goods manufactured in the city. In fairness, the city legislators argued, the tax should be apportioned statewide.

After much debate, the city's objections were overcome. The bill authorizing the construction of the canal passed the assembly by a vote of 51 to 40.

Only now the Senate had to approve the measure. Clinton knew this was where the real battle would take place. He expected Martin Van Buren to lead the fight against passage; after all, Van Buren was still fuming over Clinton's recent nomination by his party for governor and the two men barely talked. So Clinton braced himself when Van Buren took the floor.

Van Buren's speech left Clinton surprised and astonished. "Our tables have groaned with the petitions of the people," the senator announced. "We are bound to consider that the people have given their assent." And it wasn't simply this outpouring of popular support that had persuaded Van Buren. The senator went on to explain that he had come to believe the canal would greatly benefit the country's future. He urged his fellow senators to vote to allocate the funds for construction.

With Van Buren's support, the canal bill passed the Senate by 18 to 9.

THERE WAS ONE MORE legislative hurdle. Since the bill had not won by a two-thirds majority in both houses, it still could be vetoed by the Council of Revision. This body was composed of men known to be unsympathetic to the canal: the governor, the state chancellor, and three state supreme court judges.

The council's debate, however, began with the appearance of an unexpected visitor. Daniel Tompkins, the new U.S. vice president, former New York governor, and longtime Clinton enemy, arrived, glibly explaining that he just happened to be in Albany. In the past, Clinton had dismissed Tompkins as being "destitute of language, science, and magnanimity—a mere creature of accident and chance, without an iota of real greatness." As when Van Buren had taken the Senate floor, Clinton prepared himself for the expected tirade. This time he was not surprised.

The canal, Tompkins insisted, was too ambitious. It required a financial investment that was not simply huge but potentially dangerous. This money, the vice president railed, should be appropriated for military purposes. "England," he predicted, "will never forgive us for our victories. . . . We shall have another war," he said with certainty, "within two years." It would be more prudent to prepare for this inevitable war than build a canal.

It was a fiery diatribe, relentless in its opposition, passionate in its rageful call to war. And it backfired. The state chancellor, James Kent, responded, "If we must have war, or a canal, I am in favor of a canal." The other council members agreed.

The bill authorizing the construction of the canal had finally passed.

AT SUNRISE ON THE Fourth of July, 1817, a huge crowd gathered outside the city of Rome for the ceremonial groundbreaking. Speeches were applauded; cannons fired their salutes; and then Judge John Richardson, the contractor for this first section of the canal, plunged a spade into the earth. After decades of false starts and apparent dead ends, the construction of the canal had begun.

It was not easy work. Armed with only axes, shovels, and handsaws, crews of men had to create a trench four feet deep and forty feet wide through hundreds of miles of thick forest. But the workers were industrious and inventive. As they moved through the forests, they became more skilled in felling trees, inventing new methods.

Ingenuity came to the rescue, too, as the walls of the canal were constructed. When it became apparent that the lime mortar applied was inadequate, that the rising water quickly ate through the cement and caused dangerous structural cracks, a solution was found. Canvass White, a young engineer, identified a type of limestone found in Madison County that with time became increasing hard underwater. White patented his discovery in 1820. Soon this "miracle" cement was not simply used on the canal walls but was widely employed throughout the country.

Only six months after the groundbreaking, by the end of 1817, 15 miles of the canal were fully navigable. Fifty contractors had signed on, and more than a thousand men were working on the 58-mile middle section. Work, in fact, was moving ahead faster than anticipated.

The state legislature was buoyed by this progress. On April 7, 1819, the state authorized the completion of the entire canal, and the work continued to progress steadily. By 1820, the sluices were opened and water rushed in to fill the 94-mile middle section, from Utica to Montezuma. Money, too, flowed smoothly into the project. There was a great demand for the bonds, and the commission was authorized to borrow an additional $2 million.

Yet even as the canal neared completion, its speedy construction proclaimed "an engineering miracle," DeWitt Clinton's enemies decided to strike. The prospect of the canal's success propelling Clinton into the White House infuriated them. Led by Martin Van Buren, a resolution was introduced in the New York

State legislature in 1824 proposing that Clinton be removed from the Canal Commission, where he had been serving as president. The measure passed by a 24–3 vote in the assembly, and a similarly impressive 64–34 in the Senate. In a resounding vote, the legislators had stripped the "Father of the Erie Canal" of custody of his hard-won child.

When the news spread throughout the state, people were infuriated. In mass meetings in New York and Albany, the legislators were attacked and Clinton cheered. Editorials condemned Clinton's removal. Even an astonished Van Buren conceded that his rash action had mobilized "the sympathies of the people."

Clinton, opportunistic and resourceful, decided to make the most of his new popularity—and the canal's success. He ran for governor in 1824. He won by 16,359 votes, at the time a state record.

ON OCTOBER 26, 1825, Governor DeWitt Clinton boarded the *Seneca Chief* for the inaugural journey down the Erie Canal. The festive trip took eight days, and at each port cheering crowds lined up to greet the *Chief.*

When the boat made its early morning way into New York Harbor on November 4, it was followed by a procession of forty-six ships. The jubilant flotilla continued on to the mouth of the Hudson at Sandy Hook. Led by Clinton, the official delegation poured a keg of Lake Erie water slowly into the Atlantic.

On November 23, the *Seneca Chief* returned upriver to Buffalo. Judge Samuel Wilkeson, an old and faithful supporter of the canal, poured a keg of Atlantic water into Lake Erie. With that symbolic gesture, the "wedding of the waters" was consummated. The Erie Canal, a century-long vision, the longest canal in the world, a state-funded project, an engineering triumph, was finally completed.

THE CANAL WAS AN immediate success. Just twelve years after it opened, the construction debt was paid off. While from the start, its impact on the national economy was also dramatic. Largely as a result of commerce on the canal and the country's newfound ability to tap the resources in the western territories, the gross national product nearly doubled. And New York City, as predicted, also prospered, growing into a world commercial and cultural capital.

No innovation, however, lasts forever; progress demands change. With the increased competition from highways, railroads, airplanes, and other newer waterways, as the twenty-first century dawned, commercial traffic on the Erie Canal had diminished. It was no longer the lifeblood of New York's economy.

Today, though, it is still thriving—only as a recreational resource. In 2001, the Erie Canal waterways were designated the nation's twenty-third National Heritage Corridor. Sailboats and pleasure crafts now glide down its calm waters. Hikers follow its long and winding towpaths.

Nearly two hundred years after its completion, the Erie Canal remains proof that a daring government investment, guided and encouraged by tenacious and visionary leaders, can continue to reward the nation.

THREE

The Transcontinental Railroad

I N THE TWILIGHT SHADOWS, the steamer *Effie Acton* made its slow way up the Mississippi River toward the Rock Island Bridge. It was early in the evening of May 6, 1856, just days after the bridge had opened to provide a direct rail link from New York to eastern Iowa across the river. As the *Effie Acton* approached, the captain blew the whistle and, in response, the draw lumbered opened. The vessel moved easily through.

It was only after the boat had cleared the draw and veered hard to the right that things began to race out of control. The starboard engine abruptly stopped; and at the same time the port power mysteriously accelerated. The vessel slammed into the span next to the open draw.

With the collision, a stove in one of the cabins was knocked over. The fire spread rapidly. Flames engulfed the deck and flew up to the bridge's timbers. The vessel became a ball of fire, and immediately began to sink. The bridge burned through the night, and by the next day it, too, was destroyed.

It did not take long for Captain John Hurd, the owner of the *Effie Acton*, to file a suit demanding damages for the loss of his ship and his merchandise. The railroad realized, however, that more was at stake than a steamboat and its lost cargo. This court case would establish the right of railroads to bridge navigable rivers and streams—a necessity if there was ever to be a rail route across the country. The future of the railroads, of the nation's commerce, even of the country's westward expansion—all would be affected by the outcome of *Hurd* v. *Rock Island Railroad Bridge Company.*

To defend itself, the railroad needed an attorney who would not simply impugn the captain's seamanship but would forcibly make the case for rail transportation. It chose a forty-seven-year-old Illinois lawyer who had previously successfully argued the rights of the railroads to cross public lands and waters, and who had demonstrated that he was a committed advocate of rail travel.

Abraham Lincoln provided an inspired and eloquent defense. Traffic on the Mississippi, Lincoln conceded to the jury as the trial began, was important. But the future of the nation's commerce, he said, would be in moving goods from east to west. Railroads were "growing larger and larger, building up new countries with a rapidity never seen before in the history of the world." The fate of America's West, he warned in his summation, was at stake.

Lincoln—and the railroad—won the case. And this earnest lawyer's long-held support for the construction of a rail line crossing the continent, for a route uniting the east and west coasts of the nation, would be embraced with power and authority once he became president. Even as the nation fell into civil war, President Abraham Lincoln would find the vision and courage to involve the federal government in the large challenges of building and financing a transcontinental railroad across America. He would be the resolute leader who, while war raged, was also looking ahead to peace, willing to make a costly and potentially risky government investment to ensure a reunited country's prosperous future.

Yet while Lincoln's support for a rail line across America's wide plains and prairies, through its steep mountains, and over its rushing rivers and streams was crucial, the story of the building of the transcontinental railroad is a history of many men. In its long and winding path to completion, it is a tale of ambition and vision, of inventiveness and physical courage, of dreamers and crooks, of great accomplishments and great scandals. It is another American success story that demonstrates how progress comes hand-in-hand with a government's willingness to take great risks.

THEODORE JUDAH LOVED RAILROADS, and had spent his adult life building them. By the age of twenty, he had become chief engineer of the Connecticut Valley Railroad, constructing a river rail line stretching up to Vermont. He had gone on to lay a steep yet picturesque sweep of tracks along the side of a gorge high above the rapids of the Niagara River in upstate New York. And then in 1854, at twenty-eight, he was hired to build the first railroad west of the Rocky Mountains; it would be a 22-mile route to haul mining cargo through the Sacramento Valley.

It was while constructing the Sacramento Valley line that Judah found himself increasingly looking east toward the Sierra Nevada Mountains and beginning to formulate a new plan. He knew, of course, about the proposal Asa Whitney, a merchant and railroad investor, had presented nearly a decade earlier to Congress, calling for the funding of a railroad to the Pacific; that proposal had become entangled in partisan debates over routes and had eventually died. Now, however, Judah found himself staring at the Sierra Nevadas and thinking that he had found the best route to the Pacific, the one that would at last end all the discussion.

So Judah, full of energy and discipline, started work to make his vision of a rail line through the Sierra Nevadas and carrying on to the Pacific a reality. First, he began to lobby Congress. Along with his wife, Anna, he made several trips to Washington to meet with lawmakers and persuade them of both the necessity and the feasibility of his plan.

As Judah explained to the congressmen, his grueling trips from California to Washington were in themselves evidence of the need for a transcontinental railroad. There were only three ways for travelers to make the coast-to-coast journey, and each option was expensive, perilous, and time-consuming. One could travel by stagecoach—a dusty, uncomfortable, and too often dangerous six-month trip. There was the long, costly sea route around Cape

Horn. Or finally, there was treacherous passage across the yellow
fever–infected isthmus of Panama.

And while Judah knew it was important to meet with lawmak-
ers, he also recognized the need to get public support for his ideas.
In 1857, therefore, he published *A Practical Plan for Building the
Pacific Railroad.*

This manifesto insisted that the time had come to remove the
decisions about the railroad's route from politics. Instead, he argued, Congress should appoint an engineer to survey and then
plot the best route. Judah's own surveys had convinced him that
it would cost $150 million—about $75,000 a mile—to complete
the coast-to-coast rail line. This was a staggering sum in 1850s
dollars—a time when carpenters and engineers earned just $1.65
a day. Still, Judah believed that with sustained government support and leadership, private funding could be raised.

The trips to Washington and his manifesto, however, were
only preludes to Judah's most inspired act of lobbying. In 1860, Judah was given a room in the Capitol Building to present his plan
to build a railroad across the Sierra Nevadas linking California to
the eastern states. He used it to house, as he called it, "The Pacific
Railroad Museum."

And what a futuristic vision his "Museum" offered! It was a
bold, finely detailed, and often even breathtaking exhibition. He
promised "special express trains traveling across the prairies at
100 miles per hour," powerful "90-ton engines" with "14-foot driving wheels," spacious restaurant and sleeping cars.

Yet Judah shrewdly grounded his wishful dreams in facts and
figures. A series of maps—one 90 feet long—showed every inch of

the proposed path across the mountains. Each curve, bump, or obstacle was meticulously depicted. He indicated where each tunnel would need to be built, and how long it would have to be. There were drawings of the lengthy bridges that would span rivers, and detailed plans for their construction. There was even a beautifully rendered series of paintings made by his wife of the majestic Sierra Nevadas.

Congress flocked to the exhibition. Judah, who now was a celebrity, met with President James Buchanan. After their discussion, the president, an ebullient Judah rejoiced, reversed his earlier opposition. The Republicans, in fact, included Judah's proposed route—through Iowa and Nebraska, and then on to Sacramento—as a plank in their national platform for the 1860 presidential election. Their candidate, Abraham Lincoln, enthusiastically embraced it.

But Congress wanted more information. Judah was informed that before there could be even a possibility of the lawmakers approving a transcontinental railroad bill, he would need to present specific surveys demonstrating that tracks could be successfully laid over the daunting western mountains.

THE SIERRA NEVADAS WERE rough, forbidding country. The mountain route was always a challenging adventure for settlers making their way west. And there were times when it was something worse. In 1846, after a heavy snow fell on Donner Pass and blocked the passage, a stranded party of California-bound pioneers ate the remains of their dead fellow emigrants to survive.

In 1860, following his return from Washington, a disappointed, increasingly frustrated Judah found himself trekking by the Donner Pass. Dr. Daniel Strong, a druggist who lived in a nearby mining town, had asked Judah if a stage road could be built over the infamous trail; and Judah, always curious, agreed to go along and inspect. But when Judah stood on a ridge that looked down at Donner Lake, his thoughts were not about stagecoaches. He saw at once the precise route for his railroad. Tracks, he realized with excitement, would only need to cross the crest of the mountains a single time—not twice as he had plotted in the maps he had displayed in Washington.

Inspired by this time and money-saving shortcut, he and his new partner, Dr. Strong, quickly drew up papers to incorporate the Central Pacific Railroad. Only now they needed to raise the $11,500 incorporation fee required by California law.

To attract investors, Judah dashed off a pamphlet detailing his plans for a Pacific rail link through the Donner Pass. The logic of his proposal, coupled with the recent election of Lincoln, a famously ardent supporter of a transcontinental line, would, Judah felt confident, make raising money easy work. But months passed; in the end, only $7,000 had been pledged—a sizable $4,500 less than was required.

Judah refused to give up. Instead, he went to the boomtown of Sacramento to look for new, deep-pocketed investors. Collis Potter Huntington, a local merchant, and his partner, Mark Hopkins, had prospered selling tools and mining equipment to the prospectors who had flocked to California in the 1849 gold rush. Their fortunes continued to grow after canny investments in toll roads and the telegraph. Now Judah tried to persuade the two men that money could be made by supporting his railroad. As a further inducement, a desperate Judah promised that in addition to building his rail line he would also construct a wagon toll road to the Nevada mines for Huntington.

The opportunity to control a transcontinental railroad for a relatively small investment was, Huntington decided, worth the risk. He and Hopkins put up an initial $1,500, and then they raised the same amount from two other wealthy Republican Sacramento merchants, Leland Stanford and Charles Crocker.

Judah celebrated. He now had the money he needed to incorporate. But in time he would regret that he had turned to these Sacramento merchants. They would become known as the "Big Four," and they would soon be infamous for the inventiveness and scale of their corruption.

IN 1860, EVEN AS the nation moved closer to civil war, for Judah and his fellow proponents of a transcontinental railroad there was another genuine reason for optimism—Abraham Lincoln had been elected president. Besides Lincoln's having defended the railroads in court, he also had firsthand experience as a young man with railroad surveying and construction. He knew what a challenge it would be to build a line through the wilderness. Yet Lincoln was determined, as he had pledged when he was elected an Illinois state assemblyman, to be another DeWitt Clinton, a politician committed to the building of canals and railroads. Now as president, even as he found the resolve to fight a war to reunite the North and South, he was also intent on unifying the East and the West of the nation by building the Pacific railroad.

Excited by what might be accomplished with an ally in the

White House, Judah acted quickly and resourcefully. He had himself appointed the Central Pacific Railroad's federal government liaison and he went to Washington to present a new railroad bill.

Essential to Judah's bill was the chartering of *two* separate companies that would simultaneously build the lines stretching across the country. The Central Pacific (CP) would construct the California line, starting from Sacramento. The Union Pacific (UP) would lay tracks west from the Missouri River. No meeting point for the lines was designated, but an epic competition had been setup for a race across the west by the two companies.

To help build the road, the bill generously gave each of the companies a 200-foot right-of-way to lay track and 6,400 acres of land. They could also charge predetermined construction fees depending upon the terrain: $16,000 per mile over flat land; $32,000 in foothills; and $48,000 in the mountains.

After each company completed 40 miles of the line, it would receive government loans in the form of bonds in the amount of $48,000 per mile built. The entire loan—principal and interest, minus the services provided by the government—would be payable in thirty years.

It was a revolutionary bill. Cash incentives, competing companies, government bonds based on performance—nothing like this had ever been proposed before on such a vast and expensive scale. The prospect of winning congressional approval would be difficult.

There was also another complication. By 1861, the terrible enormity of the Civil War had become painfully clear to Congress. The minds and hearts of the lawmakers were focused on the great challenge of preserving the Union.

• • •

JUDAH REMAINED UNDETERRED. ADROITLY, he made valuable alliances with key elected representatives. And, another sly talent, he showed great skill in manipulating the political process.

First, he convinced Senator James McDougall of California to introduce his bill in the U.S. Senate. He had another Californian, Representative Aaron Sargent, bring it up in the House. Then, remarkably, Judah had himself named secretary of the Senate Pacific Railroad Committee, chaired by McDougall. No less shrewd of an accomplishment, he also was appointed clerk of the House subcommittee reviewing the bill.

And once the formal congressional debate began, the Civil War in its grim way proved fortuitous for Judah and his allies. With the secession of the slave states, there were no longer voices in Congress either urging a southern rail route or arguing that "states' rights" prohibited the government's building a national railway.

All of Judah's machinations, all the congressional support, would have been in vain, however, had not President Lincoln continued his vigorous support for a rail line uniting the nation. The war had not lessened his enthusiasm for the project. A coast-to-coast railroad, the president now asserted, was a strategic advantage. It would facilitate the transport of troops and war supplies. It would, Lincoln fervently believed, help to tie the western territories to the Union.

On May 6, 1862, Judah's bill passed the House by 30 votes. A month later, even after approving a substantial wartime spending bill, the Senate voted 35–5 in favor. And on June 20, 1862, a somber yet hopeful President Lincoln signed the Pacific Railroad Act into law.

BUT BEFORE CONSTRUCTION ON the Central Pacific line could begin, money had to be raised. And Judah soon discovered that while the mood in Washington was supportive, investors were less enthusiastic. Many felt that the prospect of building a railroad line across the mountains was a risky, possibly even foolish enterprise. In wartime, there were more certain profits to be made from investments in military supplies and weapons.

With little other choice, Judah once again turned to the Big Four. Each of them—calling themselves "the Associates"—bought 345 shares of Central Pacific stock. Judah and several other investors purchased lesser amounts. With this new capital, construction could at last begin.

The Big Four now controlled the railroad; they set the terms for constructing the line—and in the process ensured that they would make fortunes. Rather than distribute the work—and the fees—to independent contractors, the Big Four created their own construction company with one of their partners, Charles Crocker, as the front man. The $400,000 contract to lay the first 18 miles of CP track went to Charles Crocker & Company.

From the start, the Big Four used this new company to manipulate the provisions of the Pacific Railroad Act to collect inflated fees. Their actions were greedy, blatantly unscrupulous, and they had no trouble in routinely getting away with them. Leland Stanford, one of their own, had been elected governor and they now could act with impunity. For example, on Stanford's instructions, the California state geologist simply declared that miles of flat-lands were really foothills. This finding was endorsed by California's chief surveyor. Lincoln, with a philosophical shrug, signed off on it, too. "Here is a case in which Abraham's faith has moved mountains," the president, full of irony yet too distracted by the Civil War to fight other battles, remarked. The CP wound up receiving an additional $16,000 per mile in fees.

Judah was tormented and enraged by these practices. At a board meeting, he challenged Crocker's ability to build the line. Crocker was a merchant, not a railroad engineer, Judah charged. To appease Judah—and to avoid scrutiny of his company's business methods—Crocker agreed to relinquish his directorship. But this, too, was a calculated sham: he simply handed it to his brother.

Huntington, meanwhile, had had enough of Judah and his carping. When two new directors friendly to the Big Four were added to the CP board, Huntington made his move. He presented Judah with a challenge: Either Judah buy out the Big Four, or they would buy out Judah and his supporters.

Judah had neither the votes nor the money to oppose Huntington. He had no choice but to sell. Disconsolate, he received $1 million in CP bonds for his 500 shares.

But Judah refused to walk off in passive surrender. He was determined to regain control of the CP. He made up his mind to find the funds that would allow him to buy out Huntington and the others. Full of confidence, he soon set sail for the east coast with the hope of recruiting a group of investors that would possibly include Cornelius Vanderbilt, the steamship and railroad baron.

As Judah traveled east, a festive groundbreaking ceremony for the CP line was held on January 8, 1863. The actual construction of the line would not begin for another ten months. The first rails weren't spiked to their ties until October 26. Nearly a month later, a CP locomotive took a brief inaugural journey down a mere two miles of track.

Judah would never learn about this small first step toward the realization of his long-held and carefully nurtured dream. Weeks earlier he had died, a victim of the yellow fever he had contracted in Panama on his way to New York to find investors.

And for the Big Four, the celebration over this maiden run was short-lived. The CP was in trouble. Material and equipment, most of which needed to be shipped from the East, were proving more expensive than anticipated. Funds were rapidly running out, and new investors were not appearing. The CP was in danger of going bankrupt.

ACROSS THE COUNTRY, THE Union Pacific was having its problems, too. While the CP had been an existing company, the UP—Judah's competitive inspiration—was created by the 1862 Pacific Railroad Act. In September 1862, the first meeting of the UP commissioners was held in Chicago.

It was, at best, a dysfunctional session. Many of the commissioners opposed the building of the railroad. Half of the 163 commissioner members did not even attend the session. Arguably most detrimental of all was the absence of one man: Grenville Dodge.

In 1859, when Dodge had been a surveyor for the Illinois Central Railroad, he had heard Lincoln make a presidential campaign speech at the Pacific Hotel in Council Bluffs, Iowa. Impressed, he introduced himself to the future president. When Lincoln learned the man was a railroad expert, he immediately asked for his opinion on a westerly route.

Dodge quickly replied that tracks should be laid from Council Bluffs toward the Platte Valley.

Four years after they had met, President Lincoln summoned Dodge, now a Union general, to the White House. With the passage of the Pacific Railroad Act, the president was eager to move on the casual conversation he had had years earlier with this railroad engineer.

The bill, the president began to his old acquaintance, did not specify an eastern terminus. Any ideas? Dodge, still the champion of the Platte Valley route, advised that it should be in Omaha. The president agreed.

But Lincoln refused to go along when Dodge recommended that the government alone should build the railroad. Too many federal resources were tied up in the war, Lincoln explained. Still, Lincoln wanted Dodge—and the nation—to understand that while his beleaguered wartime administration did not have the resources to manage the building of the railroad, the government remained firmly committed to ensuring the completion of the transcontinental railroad.

Dodge continued to listen, nodding in agreement. But when Lincoln offered him the opportunity to run the UP, the general refused. Dodge explained that his commitment to a Union victory outweighed his desire to see the railroad built. "My heart," he said with a genuine passion, "is in the war."

As a consequence of Dodge's refusal, in October 1863, General John A. Dix became president of the UP board. Thomas "Doc" Durant was named the line's vice president.

It was Durant, a Wall Street trader and land speculator with a medical degree, who was the real power. He was a complicated man: shrewd, hardworking, highly competitive—and deeply corrupt. He was committed to building the railroad, and was also determined to get rich in the process.

Mimicking the CP's stunt, Durant staged an elaborate, well-publicized groundbreaking ceremony. In December 1863, crowds cheered in Omaha as shovels dug into the ground. But as was the case with the competing line, there was little genuine construction along the UP's route.

Months later, in the summer of 1864, the wily Durant, working hand-in-hand with Huntington, began an extensive campaign to persuade Congress to rewrite the 1862 Railroad Act. Their goal was to get the federal government more actively involved in the financing of the line—and in the process maximize the potential profits to investors.

Congressional critics went on the attack. They charged that further federal involvement was simply a scheme concocted by Wall Street to guarantee the investments of wealthy individuals.

But despite this arguably valid analysis, the public's support for the railroad remained both loud and firm. Letters to Congress and newspaper editorials reiterated that it was imperative to connect the eastern states to the Pacific coast.

And Lincoln's support was unwavering. The line, he said, was a national priority. He urged Congress to pass the new legislation.

Only partly in jest, the weary president remarked that he looked forward to the day when in his retirement he would ride the line all the way to California.

Durant, however, was too politically astute to count solely on the efficacy of either the president's or the public's support. He knew that ultimately Congress would need to pass the legislation, so he systematically set out to buy their votes. Bundles of UP stock were given away. Key legislators received generous contributions to their campaigns. In the end, after at least $400,000 had been spent, Durant had the votes he needed. The Railroad Act of 1864 became law.

This revised law was packed with economic incentives for the rail lines. Both the CP and the UP could now issue their own first mortgage bonds in the same amounts as the government rail bonds; they would be a quick, cheap source of new capital and as easily obtained as a second mortgage. In another helpful change, the lines no longer had to lay 40 miles of track before they would receive their first payments; now the funds would be released after just 20 miles. And for every mile of track, the lines would receive a munificent land grant of 12,800 acres. Even better, the companies were given the right to mine coal and iron on their vast new tracts of lands.

If the tracks could be laid, if the railroad could be built, there now was the opportunity for the men who controlled the lines to become wealthy beyond any previous expectations.

WORK ON THE CP continued, but the line was still struggling. By March 1864, the company had, in a rather haphazard way, laid down the first 22 miles of track. After the new Railroad Act became law, another 20 miles was more efficiently put down. But problems remained, and continued to threaten the entire enterprise.

Money was the first. The initial 36 miles had cost the CP $3 million, and by the end of 1864 the company was nearly broke. Even when the California legislature voted to guarantee the CP's bond interest, there were relatively few buyers for the bonds. Another complication, the federal government was slow in paying monies and delivering land promised by the 1864 bill. And large future expenses loomed. The cost to tunnel through the Sierra Nevadas would be staggering.

Laborers were a second problem. By the spring of 1865, there were 2,500 men working on the line. That was a woefully insufficient force if the CP was to move east from California and into the steep mountains. But the line could not afford to hire any new men.

With a lack of capital, with a shortage of workers, the CP was beginning to suspect that it was doomed. But then, providentially, money began to pour in. A court ordered the city of San Francisco to pay the company a contested $400,000 in stocks and bonds. The government released a $1.25 million payment that had been inexplicably held up for a year; and, as specified in the new Railroad Act, the company could borrow against these funds. Additionally, a small stretch of the California CP rail line opened and began to bring in revenues.

These new funds allowed the Big Four finally to address their other major problem—the shortage of workers. But although the company could now afford to hire new laborers, it still could not attract them. The pay was too low, the hours too long, the tasks too dangerous. No one, it seemed, wanted the job.

CHARLIE CROCKER HAD AN idea. There were, he estimated, about 60,000 Chinese immigrants in California. Nearly all of them were adult males, and few were employed. The CP, he suggested, should hire them.

The head of the line's labor force, James Harvey Strobridge, argued against his boss's suggestion. Chinese men were too small and frail, he admonished. They would not be able to do the demanding physical work.

Crocker countered by reminding Strobridge of the Great Wall. It was built by Chinese workers.

Strobridge capitulated. He agreed to hire fifty Chinese laborers for one month as a test. Besides, he conceded, there was no other option; nobody else wanted the work.

That first month was a revelation to Strobridge. He had to admit that the Chinese were tireless and skillful. Instinctively, they worked in teams, were quick to learn how to blast rocks, and were careful to avoid injuries. He agreed that more Chinese should be employed.

The CP hired every Chinese immigrant who wanted the job. When this was not sufficient, Crocker turned to a San Francisco labor contractor for help and instructed him to locate 2,000 additional "coolies." Import them from China if necessary, Crocker ordered.

And so shiploads of Chinese immigrants arrived in California to work on the railroad. Boys as young as thirteen and men as old as sixty were hired. By the end of 1865, 7,000 Chinese were building the line—a total that was more than three times the number of Caucasians in the CP workforce.

Their presence did not go unnoticed. News reports praised their personal thrift, their adroitness, and their natural skills. But in all the flurry of laudatory articles, there was little mention of the great dangers these workers were routinely required to face. Or the large number of Chinese men who lost their lives during construction.

Cape Horn, for example, was a steep three-mile gorge at the North Fork of the American River. The route east required that tracks be built along a ledge 1,300 feet above the valley floor. Lowered by ropes, the workers drilled by hand into the sheer cliffs, placed their explosives, and then had to scurry up the ropes before the charges detonated. It was daring, complicated work; and many were killed in the process.

The challenges in building the seven tunnels needed for the line to traverse the Donner Summit were even more perilous. The men were lowered down eight-by-twelve-foot shafts to blast away rock. There was a constant cacophony of explosions; hundreds of barrels of black powder were ignited each day. Once the tunnels had been carved, work inside was suffocating and brutal. Above and underground, accidents were commonplace. Men died each day.

But the work continued, and new tracks were laid. By the fall of 1866, the Chinese workers had pushed the line 92 miles east of Sacramento. By August 1867, the crews had blasted through the

Donner Summit. After five years of construction, the CP resolutely had made its way through the route's most forbidding terrain.

The CP could now lay down its track more rapidly—and, the Big Four hoped, outpace its rival in the race across America.

BACK EAST, THE UP was busy, too. But most of the company's activities seemed to be focused on taking advantage of the provisions in the new Railroad Act. Land grants, mineral rights, hefty subsidies for construction—all were legislated and legitimate benefits of railroad construction. "The real money to be made," Doc Durant, the UP's vice president, realized with an undisguised glee, "was in constructing the road, not operating it." He conspired with a swashbuckling entrepreneur, George Francis Train, to take full and often inventive advantage of this opportunity.

The two men bought a dormant company named the Pennsylvania Fiscal Agency and, hoping to give it a more impressive imprimatur, renamed it Crédit Mobilier of America. Then Durant used his position with the railroad to award the construction contract to Crédit Mobilier.

But Durant and Train still were not satisfied. Crédit Mobilier charged the railroad tens of millions of dollars more than the actual costs. And because Durant and Train controlled both companies, no one could very well prevent this scheme. The two men, in effect, took the money that was coming into one of their corporations and then stuffed it into another company they ran.

For example, the UP agreed to pay Crédit Mobilier $50,000 per mile in building costs. This sum was quite a generous windfall, but Durant was not satisfied. The longer the route, he reasoned, the more money could be made. Therefore, he simply ordered the railroad to follow an oxbow-shaped route rather than a straight one. And Crédit Mobilier—his company, too!—could collect an additional half-million dollars.

These tactics did not go unnoticed. Peter Dey, the UP chief engineer, was infuriated. According to historian Stephen Ambrose, Dey fumed about Durant: "If geography was a little larger, I think he would order a survey round by the moon and a few of the fixed stars to see if he could get more depot grounds."

By the end of 1864 not a single tie had been laid on the UP line, but a fortune had been raised by Crédit Mobilier. Dey could no longer tolerate the underhanded deals Durant had been making. He resigned.

Durant was not insulted. In fact, he felt exultant: he had removed his main detractor. Now he could concentrate on building the line—and funneling more money into Crédit Mobilier.

But to build the line, UP still desperately needed construction funds. Once again, Lincoln took control, using his prestige and authority to set in motion a plan that would help guarantee the railroad's success.

On January 20, 1865, the president summoned Oakes Ames, a wealthy Massachusetts congressman, to the Oval Office. He told Ames that the line must be built and that Ames was the man who could get it done. If Ames succeeded in completing the UP, the president shrewdly suggested, the congressman's legacy would be assured.

Ames was flattered, and intrigued. He and his brother Oliver bought $1 million in Crédit Mobilier stock and loaned $600,000 to the UP. Durant now had the funds to move forward with construction.

Yet before a single spike could be driven, the Civil War ended and Lincoln was assassinated. With the unexpected death of its powerful champion in April 1865, the future of the UP line was suddenly in jeopardy.

THE CESSATION OF THE hostilities, however, brought several benefits. Money was now freed to invest in the line. Decommissioned soldiers could find civilian jobs building the railroad. And, no less consequentially, when Grenville Dodge was offered the position as the UP's chief engineer, he now eagerly took it.

Dodge threw himself into organizing and guiding the building of the line. He gave returning veterans of the war a steady wage, shelter (of a sort), and in return demanded ten- and eleven-hour work days. Men signed on, and tracks began being rapidly laid. By July 1866, the UP had completed the first 100 miles of track required by the 1864 law.

As the work progressed, money once again began to run out. Congressman Ames decided to raise new capital by selling shares to his fellow lawmakers and to his Boston friends. This worked so well that the Ames group soon controlled the majority of Crédit Mobilier stock, and Oliver Ames became president of the UP. A pitched battle was brewing with Durant over control of the railroad.

While corporate strife threatened to rip the company apart, a new problem arose. By the summer of 1867, the line had moved westward into Indian territory. The Native Americans feared with good reason that the western migration of the White Man would be a threat to their way of live. When civilization encroached, they would lose their lands and their hunting grounds. So the tribes attacked. Anyone affiliated with the railroad and its construction was the enemy. With a calculated fury, the Indians swooped down on railroad crews and killed as many as they could.

Dodge turned to the U.S. Army and his old boss, General William Tecumseh Sherman, for help. He demanded that the Army respond with massive force and exterminate the Indians.

Sherman refused; he wanted to try for a peaceful settlement. But when the negotiations made little progress, the railroad grew impatient. It organized its own force of Indian fighters to drive off the attacking tribes.

All the while, the laying of tracks continued. After five years of sustained construction, the UP line stretched 530 miles west of Omaha. It had laid more than five times as much track as the CP.

A gloating Durant sent a telegram to Leland Stanford highlighting his line's success. The message was meant to be intimidating, but it had the opposite effect. The CP was energized, and announced its determination to outdo the rival line.

Durant accepted the challenge. "I'll be damned," he barked, "if I would not prevent the CP from coming more than 200 miles east of California."

Finally, in 1868, the competition that Congress had envisioned when it had authorized the two separate lines was under way.

IT WAS A RACE to the finish. And the stakes were high. The company that could lay the most track would be granted tens of thousands of acres of land and the accompanying mineral rights, as well as a fortune in government bonds. But pride, too, was a factor. Both railroads had struggled for years, and both wanted to be declared the winner—the company which had built the longest line.

The CP had emerged from the Sierras, and had moved into the relatively flat land of the Nevada desert. The heat was broiling, but the CP pushed its workers. More than six miles of rail were laid each day. Men died from exhaustion and dehydration. But the CP pressed on, heading east.

The UP officials heard about the progress the rival line was making, and this made them push their own men, too. And the UP had an advantage. Supplies shipped from the east coast made their way with relative ease to the company. Merchandise shipped to the CP had to be sent aboard boats that journeyed around the Horn. It was all too common for entire shipments of vital CP cargoes to be lost in these treacherous seas.

As the race across America intensified, the two desperate companies wantonly began to cut corners. Three UP bridges collapsed and the construction on the CP line was similarly shoddy. The newspapers started out by attacking these building practices and then, smelling investigative blood, moved on to examine how both companies conducted their financial business. "There is cheating on the grandest scale in all these railroads," the *New York Herald* charged. And people began to listen.

Each company now realized that the nation might soon lose its patience with an enterprise that had gone on too long and had made illegitimate fortunes for too many. Each understood that the time had come to bring the work to an end.

First, however, they had to agree on a termination point. None of the legislation had ever established where the two lines should meet. Both companies had their own agendas and preferences, and for years their suggestions had been fiercely debated. But now as opposition to the railroads was building, the companies understood that it was in both lines' best interests to reach a pragmatic settlement. The CP and UP agreed to connect their lines at the summit of the Promontory Mountains in Utah.

On May 10, 1869, the Central Pacific engine *Jupiter* and the Union Pacific's engine *No. 119* steamed toward each other along the Utah mountain tracks. They moved nose-to-nose, and then stopped. Engineers from both companies reached across the space between the two engines and shook hands. Simultaneously, a telegraph signal was sent out around the country: The railroad uniting the nation from coast to coast was completed.

THE COSTS OF THIS enterprise were huge and traumatic. Chinese workers died by the hundreds. Native Americans were massacred, and for the survivors their cherished way of life fell into ruin. The rapacious scheming and colossal fraud of the CP and UP companies as well as Credit Mobilier earned illicit fortunes.

But the transcontinental railroad also proved to be a shrewd investment for the government. The financial gamble had been tremendous. The federal government had initially loaned the two companies a total of more than $64 million. Yet by 1869, when the railroads had settled up, the government had earned a profit of more than $103 million on its loans.

More significant, as courageous leaders such as Lincoln and

steadfast visionaries such as Judah had predicted, the creation of the transcontinental railroad transformed the nation. People rode the train west, and towns and great cities sprung up along the way. The country spread out, and prospered. A wise and daring investment, nurtured by men of courage and determination, had helped America to fulfill its destiny.

FOUR

The Land Grant Colleges

A T FIFTEEN, JUSTIN MORRILL left school. He had hoped to go to college, to study philosophy and perhaps even law, but he could not afford the fees. With regret and resignation, the teenager instead found work in his Vermont town as a clerk for a local merchant.

Although he never had a college education, Morrill, full of ambition and common sense, went on to achieve a measure of success. And in 1852, at forty-two, he was elected to Congress.

But neither the passing of the years nor his accomplishments lessened the sense of disappointment Morrill felt over his failure to earn a college diploma. In fact, he had come to believe that his lost opportunity—and that of the thousands of other young men and women who could not afford to continue their education—was also a lost opportunity for the nation. If America were to realize its founding democratic principle of equality, if the nation were to capitalize on the intellectual excellence necessary for the new industrial era, then its colleges needed to be open to all who were qualified. Further, it was the obligation of both the federal and state governments to work in a financial partnership with educational institutions. It was an investment, Morrill perceptively believed, that a responsible nation had to make—and one that would pay munificent dividends to the country as well as to the students. And now that Morrill was in Congress he was determined to make a college education a broadly available benefit of American life.

The story of Justin Morrill's campaign to create a network of government-funded colleges in each state that would be open to students from all social classes is another case study of how an iron-willed political leader can persevere over narrow-minded critics to persuade lawmakers to make a substantial and costly contribution to the country's infrastructure.

Yet it would be wrong to reflect on Morrill's legislative accomplishment as merely an example of spirited dealmaking or wily politics. The Morrill Act of 1862 was, most fundamentally, another far-seeing national investment inspired by one of the republic's founding ideals: The enemy of American success is not failure but the lack of opportunity.

EVEN BEFORE THE BIRTH of the republic, there was a growing mood in the colonies that in the New World education should not be a privilege available only to an elite. In Europe, education had been open only to the ruling classes. It was one more way those with advantages institutionalized and passed on their power and prosperity. Life in America, the colonists hoped, would be different. In the New World, what once were privileges would be deemed inalienable rights.

Starting in 1743, Benjamin Franklin began publishing essays maintaining that freedom and equality were intrinsically intertwined with education. A free society, he wrote, must be an educated society. In his *Proposals Relating to the Education of Youth in Pennsylvania*, published in 1750, Franklin, the instinctive democrat, urged that schooling be provided to all children in the colonies, not merely the sons and daughters of the rich.

In the Old World, religious beliefs were another exclusionary standard for education. In America, this, too, was being reevaluated. When a group of Baptist clergy in 1764 chartered Rhode Island College (now Brown University), it was part of the founding credo that students of all religious beliefs be accepted. But Franklin's Academy and College of Philadelphia (now the University of Pennsylvania), founded in 1740, was the first non-sectarian institution of higher education in the colonies. Its curriculum was also radical: it was not designed to educate the clergy, but to provide a practical education in the arts as well as the skills to make a living.

After the Revolution, the belief in public education—a tenet of personal freedom and a boom to the national prosperity—became part of the young republic's idealistic policy. At the Continental Congress in 1783, Colonel Thomas Pickering lectured his fellow lawmakers that "schools and the means of education shall forever be encouraged." Two years later, the Congress finally responded to Pickering's ardent speeches. It passed a law that was visionary, egalitarian, and precedential: in each town, a plot of land must be reserved to establish an institution for public education.

WITH THE LOUISIANA PURCHASE, the construction of the Erie Canal, and the prospect of a transcontinental railroad, as the nineteenth century moved forward the young nation was beginning to have intimations of its future prosperity and greatness. But America was also still largely an illiterate, rural, and agrarian country. If it were to achieve its potential destiny, it would need to have a better-educated citizenry.

This education, American freethinkers urged, should be practical as well as intellectual. The European elitist curriculum with its stolid emphasis on ancient texts would, many felt, be too esoteric in a gung-ho land where hard work and ambition could, at least in theory, propel any young white man to success. A Yale student of that era complained that "the minds of the students were being developed in the same manner as are the livers of the geese at Strasburg—every day sundry spoonfuls of the same mixture forced down all throats alike." In a New World founded on democratic principles, in an emerging economy driven by a roll-up-your-sleeves competitiveness and innovation, such educational practices were not just antiquated but increasingly irrelevant. Knowledge would be the egalitarian pathway to success in America—but only if it were utilitarian, a way of earning a living.

And so at the beginning of the nineteenth century when President Thomas Jefferson advocated universal education to Congress, he emphasized the pragmatic nature of his proposed American curriculum: courses in agriculture, practical science, and the military arts. "A public institution can alone supply those sciences which are ... necessary to complete the circle, all the parts of which contribute to the improvement of the country, and some of them to its preservation," he said. But the truly innovative part of the educational plan Jefferson presented to Congress in 1806 was his proposal that a nationwide network of colleges be built on land donated by the federal government.

Fearful of the expense, still not convinced of either the inevitability or the scope of the changes that would accompany the Industrial Revolution, Congress rejected Jefferson's plan. However, with that presidential initiative the revolutionary principle of government financial support for higher education entered into the national dialogue.

Within decades, a variety of plans were presented to lawmakers outlining the establishment of a national system of colleges. Nearly all of them shared one identical provision: as the population moved westward, the proceeds from the sale of public lands should be used to fund institutions of higher education. Professor Jonathan Baldwin Turner's 1851 *Plan for a State University for the Industrial Classes*, for example, called for experimental agriculture research stations, a nationwide network of government supported institutions of practical learning—and all would be constructed on land donated by Washington.

Congress, however, remained reluctant to authorize a federal investment of such scope and expense, especially when the returns could not be measured in such tangible commodities as dollars and cents. Lawmakers needed to be convinced (and cajoled) into believing that a better-educated America would be a greater America; and that the money spent would be a remarkably economical investment in the country's rich future.

JUSTIN MORRILL TRIED, AND he failed. In 1856, after being elected as a Republican to his second term in the House of Representatives, he offered up a cautiously modest education bill. He proposed the creation of "one or more national agricultural schools" where one student from each district and two from each state could "receive a scientific and practical education at the public expense." But the concept of "education at the public expense" was too radical for a Congress still dominated by a privileged majority of legislators who had been educated at expensive private institutions.

Morrill, however, refused to give up. Goaded on by a self-made man's confidence, he kept hammering away at his fellow lawmakers. He introduced a more expansive version of his bill in 1857; and then, when that failed to gain approval, he proposed an even more radical draft the following year. He explained his support with a fiery speech in April 1858 that would quickly become famous as a call to action.

At a time when the nation was considering spending a fortune to build railroads, Morrill began, it was also necessary to shore up a once very profitable but now declining segment of the nation's economy—agriculture. If agricultural output continued to suffer, the congressman warned, then so would the national income. And, no less ominous, with the decrease in agricultural exports, the national debt would grow, holding the country in its "thralldom."

But there was a way to reverse this economic spiral—with education and training. Morrill argued for the "propriety of encouraging useful knowledge among farmers and mechanics in order to enlarge our productive power." Just as the country had schools to teach the art of war, it needed practical institutions to "teach men the way to feed, clothe, and enlighten the great brotherhood of man." Four fifths of the population at the time, Morrill stated, were "engaged in agricultural or mechanical employment. Is it not of grave importance to give this vast force an intelligent direction?" he challenged.

Full of passion, Morrill also insisted that it was the duty—a moral responsibility—of the federal government to provide this "intelligent" education to its citizens. His bill, he conceded, would pass on to the states a total of about 5.8 million acres that would be used for colleges. But even after this distribution, Morrill thundered, the federal government would still own more than 1 billion acres.

In the House, Ohio congressman George Pugh charged that Morrill's College Land Bill involved "as atrocious a violation of the organic laws as if it were the act of an armed usurper." The chairman of the Committee on Public Lands opposed it, too. Yet the bill squeaked by, 105 to 100.

The Senate debate was dominated by states' rights southerners. A fuming James Mason of Virginia declared that the bill was "one of the most extraordinary engines of mischief . . . a misuse of federal property" and "an unconstitutional robbing of the Treasury." Clement Clay of Alabama raged that it was "monstrous" and "iniquitous." But senators from the northern and western states prevailed and again the bill narrowly passed, 25 to 22.

Only now President Buchanan, yielding to the southern Democrats, vetoed the bill. Frustrated, Morrill had no choice but to accept that his bill could not be reconsidered until there was a new president.

WITH THE ELECTION OF Lincoln in 1860, Morrill glumly realized the times were still not propitious. Congress was preoccupied with the looming threat of a bloody and expensive civil war. Support for the transcontinental railroad was also growing among the lawmakers; this, too, would be a demanding enterprise, involving colossal expenditures. But Morrill would not be deterred.

In 1862, he introduced the Morrill Act, or, as it became known, the Land Grant College Act. The nation was at war, the future of the Union was uncertain, yet Morrill stood on the floor of the House and spoke with full confidence in the necessity for immediate action on his egalitarian plan:

This bill proposes to establish at least one college in every state upon a sure and perpetual foundation, accessible to all, but especially to the sons of the soil, where all of needful science for the practical avocations of life shall be taught; where neither the higher graces of classical studies nor that military drill our country now so greatly appreciates will be ignored; and where agriculture, the foundation of all present and future prosperity, may look for troops of earnest

*friends, studying its familiar and recondite economics, and
at last elevating it to that higher level where it may fearlessly
invoke comparison with the most advanced standards of the
world.*

It was a bill demanding that a federal government besieged by
a wrenching war not only turn its focus to the future, but also voluntarily surrender territory. Each state would receive 30,000 acres
for each member of Congress the state had as of the 1860 census;
a total of 11.5 million acres would be transferred to the states by
this formula.

Nevertheless, the wartime Congress understood Morrill's economic logic: the land grants would not be an expenditure, but an
investment. And with the secession of the southern states, Morrill's
most vitriolic opponents had left Washington. The bill passed both
the House and the Senate.

The decision now rested with President Lincoln. It was
Lincoln's great gift that even as he guided the nation through a terrible conflict whose outcome was uncertain, even as he was mired
in the demanding responsibilities of a wartime commander in
chief, he had the wisdom to look toward the nation's greater future. On July 2, 1862, Lincoln signed Morrill's bill into law.

ONLY NOW, THERE WAS a problem Morrill had not foreseen: Students did not want to go to the land grant colleges. After the end
of the Civil War, even after a second Land Grant Act in 1890 extended the program to sixteen southern states, the new institutions still had difficulty attracting students.

Part of the reason was that a college education—*any* college education—continued to be viewed by many as a luxury, even an indulgence. In 1870, only about 50,000 students in the entire country were enrolled in higher education; that was less than 2 percent of the potential college-age population. Even as the land grant colleges were opening, other institutions, unable to find students, were closing their doors. Or, as was the case with Harvard's Lawrence Scientific School and MIT, many were forced to merge in order to survive. Throughout the country, the number of available college scholarships was greater than the number of applicants.

Also unanticipated by Morrill was the hostility of America's farmers. They simply did not believe there was a need for a scientific agricultural education. As James B. Angell, president of the Michigan Agricultural College, despaired in an 1869 essay: "The great insuperable trouble is to inspire farmers with the belief that science has anything to offer them."

But it wasn't just the lack of students that was undermining the new land grant schools. It was also the challenge, the college administrators quickly discovered, to find faculty staff with the requisite knowledge to teach a scientific approach to farming. One frustrated college president complained: "To find men possessed of these qualities is difficult in any branch. It is doubly difficult in a branch in which science is in its infancy and in which very few men have had any scientific training."

The greatest obstacle, however, to the success of the land grant schools were the nation's "classical" colleges. These schools, which had been chartered decades before the passage of Morrill's bill, saw the new institutions as their competitors for what had historically been a relatively small number of students. Snobbery played a petulant role, too. The old colleges, one observer noted, "looked askance upon the new intruders into their prescriptive domain."

When in 1872 a bill to increase the land grants came up for debate in Congress, Presidents James McCosh of Princeton and Charles Eliott of Harvard intensely lobbied against it. They argued that the land grant colleges were an unnecessary drain on the national budget, especially since, they maintained, the European experience had demonstrated that agriculture could not be taught in the classroom.

Fueled by this opposition, the bill was defeated. And so, it seemed, was the future of the land grant colleges.

YET AS IT BECAME apparent to farmers that science could help produce bigger crops and greater productivity, as the intellectual demands of the Industrial Revolution increased the need for engineers, the enrollments at the land grant colleges slowly began to increase. And as these colleges prospered, higher education was made available to new segments of the nation—the working classes, women, minorities, and immigrants. Morrill's vision of an America where an activist and democratic government took the responsibility to provide the opportunity for a college diploma to a broad segment of the population was becoming a reality.

Today, the land grant colleges are an essential part of American academic life. Over 3 million students are enrolled each year in the nation's 104 land grant institutions. To date, they have collectively awarded 20 million diplomas. And their partnership with the federal and state government has also flourished: the endowments to states for these colleges is collectively more than $550 million annually.

These are stunning achievements. America is a nation whose strength and wealth are built on opportunity, knowledge, innovation, and excellence—a prosperity that would have been impossible without Morrill's unflagging tenacity and fair-minded vision.

The Homestead Act

A N ENTHUSIASTIC, OVERFLOWING CROWD eager to hear the young congressman from Tennessee swarmed into New York's City Hall on May 27, 1852. George Henry Evans, the writer who had popularized the slogan "Vote Yourself a Farm," and his friend Horace Greeley, the editor of the widely read *New York Tribune*, who had famously advised "Go West, young man, and grow up with the country" took seats amidst the curious sea of people. They, too, wanted to take measure of the man who had championed their cause and done the seemingly impossible: he had persuaded the House of Representatives to pass a bill granting "free" land to homesteaders.

Andrew Johnson did not disappoint his audience. He had had

no formal schooling; it was his wife who had taught him to read and write. Before turning to politics, he had been a tailor. But Johnson had a natural eloquence, a keen mind, and a heartfelt belief in the principle that "every poor man in the United States" was entitled to a tract of public land "without money and without price." When he spoke, he energized the crowd and had them on their feet cheering. He charmed them, too. When a voice hissed disapprovingly, a grinning Johnson paused to reprimand that only two creatures hiss—a viper from the malignity of its own venom, and a goose because of its stupidity.

Elated, Evans and Greeley left the lecture convinced that with Johnson's stewardship it would not be long before the legislation became law. However, before the year was over, Johnson's congressional seat was gerrymandered away by a vindictive Tennessee legislature and he was out of office. "I have no political future," he moaned. The prospects for the Homestead Act were similarly bleak.

Johnson, though, would not give up either on politics or his belief that it was in the country's best interest to offer settlers vacant plots of publicly owned western land. His steely determination over two decades to make the Homestead Act a law is another example of how a committed leader can mobilize a reluctant and politically divided Congress to make large and costly investments in the country's future. It is also further proof that wise and idealistic federal initiatives can strengthen the national character as they help to create a more prosperous America.

• • •

AMERICA WAS GROWING. AS the young country charged through the nineteenth century, its boundaries spread bountifully. The Louisiana Purchase in 1803, the annexation of Texas in 1845, the establishment of the Oregon Territory in 1846, the Mexican secession of its northern lands in 1848—all dramatically expanded the republic. Stretching from the Atlantic to the Pacific, from Canada in the north to Mexico in the south, America had become a big country.

Yet, while the nation now spread across a vast and diverse landscape, its population remained concentrated in the eastern states. This was a dangerous disparity. It was strategically crucial that people protect, defend, and Americanize the far corners of the republic.

No less significant for the country, this was also a defining situation. If only a wealthy elite were allowed to purchase the new lands, if vast tracts became personal fiefdoms, if opportunities for the poor and the working class were eliminated in the West, then the founding constitutional ideals of equality and opportunity would be undermined. America could in time be transformed into a restrictive nation where one's status at birth largely predetermined one's fate.

The settlement of these territories, however, could also work to reinforce the country's democratic character. As James Madison wrote in *Federalist Paper* No. 10, extending "the sphere" of a nation meant that "you take in a greater variety of parties and interests; you make it less probable that a majority of the whole will have a common motive to invade the rights of other citizens."

The fledgling nation was once again at a turning point. Territorial expansion brought with it responsibilities and challenges. And the nature of America's response would help determine its destiny.

AS EARLY AS 1797, settlers along the Ohio River had turned to the national government for assistance. Land was abundant, but the newcomers could not afford to purchase homesteads. So with great hopes, they petitioned Congress: Grant each family 400 acres for a farm, and after three years of cultivation the deeds to these federally owned tracts would be transferred to the farmers. It was a suggestion, the pioneers were convinced, that would benefit both an expanding nation and its citizens. Congress, however, refused. Year after year the proposal was resubmitted, and each time it was denied. In Mississippi and Indiana, other homesteading plans were also sent to Washington and also summarily rejected.

But despite these setbacks, the Ohio settlers continued to pressure Congress. Hoping to maximize their efficacy, they organized in 1812 into the True American Society and sent a new, almost plaintive appeal to the federal lawmakers. The Ohio pioneers were "poor and suffering, while thousands of acres of land, the property of the United States, are laying unoccupied," their petition complained. This emotional outcry from his constituents persuaded Ohio senator James Morrow to introduce a bill calling for the granting of homesteads. But Congress remained unaffected. The bill never moved beyond the Committee on Public Lands.

That same year, though, as the nation became embroiled in

the War of 1812, anxious lawmakers passed the Military Tract of 1812. This wartime legislation contained an important provision that, in time, would prove precedential for the homesteader's cause. It set aside "bounty lands"—parcels of federal property that would be given to soldiers as both incentives and payments for military service.

When the war ended, this pragmatic approach to the distribution of public land influenced and helped shape Missouri senator Thomas Hart Benton's inventive land use legislation. In 1825, he offered a bill that, he felt, would appeal to the two definitive strands in the emerging national character—that "of a mere financier" and that "of a statesman."

Owning land, Benton believed, was the natural and inalienable right of every American settler. But he shrewdly recognized that a Congress filled with wealthy lawmakers did not share his populist philosophy. So, his plan offered a balanced compromise.

To appease the capitalists, Benton proposed that "the best of the land" be sold "for prices adapted to its value." Squatters would not automatically be given an unconditional right to purchase the land they occupied. They would simply have "first right," and only at the market value. Prices, however, would be reduced the longer land stayed on the market.

To appease the homesteaders, Benton outlined "a plan for the gratuitous donation of the remainder." Unsold land would become "refuse land" and be freely distributed by Congress. "The settler in a new country," the senator argued, "pays the value of the best land in the privations he endures, in the hardship he encounters, and in the labor he performs."

Benton's even-handed attempt at a compromise to resolve the fate of the land in the new territories did not have immediate legislative success. Congress adamantly rejected his bill.

But now the public was listening. Largely as a result of the Missouri senator's bill, influential segments of the electorate began to think seriously and write passionately about homesteading.

IT WAS A PUBLIC campaign and it demonstrated the power of the pen to shape and dramatize a national movement. George Henry Evans was a founder of the National Reform Association and his articles appeared regularly in the *Working Man's Advocate*. Horace Greeley was the founder and editor of the popular *New York Tribune*. Writing with both an ardent militancy and an earnest reasonableness, the two men waged a sustained campaign to make homesteading a national right. Individual land ownership, they argued with a democratic certitude, was an essential part of American life. Further, the practical benefits would be twofold: while there were few available jobs in the overpopulated East, workers would find countless opportunities for employment in the West; and a westward migration would also create a new demand for manufactured goods.

Voters must elect lawmakers who understood the need for a homestead act, the two writers urged. "Vote Yourself a Farm," Evans, with a catchy simplicity, instructed. The more didactic Greeley offered a fully reasoned call for action in his 1850 book, *Hints Toward Reforms*. "A single law of Congress," he wrote, "proffering to each landless citizen a patch of the Public Domain . . . and forbidding farther sale of the Public Lands, except in limited quantities . . . would promote immensely the independence, morality, industry, and comfort of our entire laboring population evermore."

It was an effective argument. And it caught the attention of the relatively new Free Soil Party. Shrewdly, partly members adopted the free distribution of land to settlers as one of their tenets. At the party's 1848 convention, where former president Martin Van Buren was chosen as its presidential candidate, the platform emphatically endorsed homesteading: "Resolved, the free grant to actual settlers, in consideration of the expenses they incur in making settlements in the wilderness . . . is a wise and just measure of public policy which will promote, in various ways, the interests of all the states in the Union."

Van Buren did not win a single vote in the Electoral College. He did, however, garner a substantial nationwide popular vote. And with his campaign, the issue of free land became an even more significant part of the national dialogue.

Four years later, in 1852, when the Free Soil Party nominated John Hale as its presidential candidate, the platform embraced homesteading with an even greater fervor:

> . . . All men have a natural right to a portion of the soil; and that, as the use of soil is indispensable to life, the right of all men to the soil is as sacred as their right to life. That public lands of the United States belong to the people, and should not be sold to individuals nor granted to corporations, but should be held as a sacred trust for the benefit of the people, and should be granted in limited quantities, free of cost, to landless settlers.

The Free Soil Party's campaign as well as the sustained appearance of hard-hitting editorials and essays began to influence Congress. A bit. No definitive homesteading act was proposed, but lawmakers did sponsor legislation that endorsed the concept of the free distribution of public lands. Bills were passed, for example, that offered land grants to frontiersmen in Florida, Oregon, Washington, and New Mexico in return for protecting the nation against hostile Indians. Another statute rewarded land to settlers in Oregon who acted to discourage the British efforts to gain control of the territory. And Representative William Smith of Alabama offered up a pointedly crude, mean-spirited yet nevertheless effective argument to his fellow lawmakers in the 32nd Congress: It is "the duty of Congress to help the cities disgorge their cellars and their garrets of . . . useless population" and send these undesirables westward.

But it was not until Andrew Johnson stepped onto the national stage that all the diverse arguments, all the heartfelt political movements, and all the well-chosen published words began to produce tangible legislative results. His single-minded efforts to pass the Homestead Act would drag on for decades; but in the end the tenacious Johnson would accomplish what other men could not.

ANDREW JOHNSON'S TAILOR SHOP in Greenville, Tennessee, had become the community's meeting place. Workers, farmers, artisans—all manners of people in this small southern town would congregate at Johnson's shop to discuss the issues of the day and, not least, to listen to Johnson. He was a mesmerizing talker, a man who could win any argument, and a man who never failed to speak his mind. He even dared to oppose the slaveholding aristocracy. When people urged him to run for office, Johnson listened. He was elected in 1828 as an alderman, then he became mayor, and in 1837 he moved on to the state senate.

In 1839, as a state senator, he began his campaign for land settlement. Speaking to the Tennessee legislature, he declared that the selling of public land would both generate revenue for the federal government and at the same time be an investment in the future: the benefits to the nation from the cultivation of its vast, vacant territories would be enormous.

When Johnson arrived in Washington, D.C., in 1843 as a congressman, he continued to argue for the distribution of federal land to settlers. In 1846, full of confidence and a deep belief in the rightness of his cause, Johnson introduced the first Homestead bill. "Every poor man in the United States who is the head of a family," the bill stated, could receive 160 acres "without money and without price."

Johnson's fellow southerners immediately went on the attack. Homesteading, they responded, would be of little use to slaveholders who required vast tracts of land for their plantations rather than a mere 160 acres. And what about the loss of potential revenue from land sales? The federal government, the southern congressmen argued, needed this income.

Congress voted down Johnson's bill. Undeterred, he reintroduced homesteading legislation in the Congress of 1848–49. When that bill also failed, the tenacious Johnson simply reintroduced it a year later. "Pass this bill," he appealed with genuine passion, and each representative "would feel that he had filled the full object of his mission here, and could return home to his constituents in quiet and peace." Despite Johnson's ardor, the bill was defeated.

Frustrated, Johnson still refused to give up. Shrewdly, he looked for support outside Congress and began corresponding regularly with homesteading advocates throughout the country. It was a strategy that was both symbiotic and beneficial. His letters to Horace Greeley, for example, encouraged the editor to continue to write about the issue. At the same time, Greeley's manifestos helped to persuade Johnson that there was public support for homesteading and that he should continue to petition Congress. With that encouragement, Johnson once again brought his bill before the House of Representatives. In December 1852, the House voted 105–57 to pass his Homesteading Act.

Even with this victory, Johnson knew that other obstacles remained. It would be difficult to get the bill through the Senate. And even if he had the senators' approval, there was certainly no guarantee the president would sign the bill. Johnson had not, however, anticipated what would happen next. The Tennessee legislature gerrymandered Johnson's congressional district; he could not win reelection. Without a seat in Congress, Johnson would have neither the power nor the position to lead the fight to make the Homesteading Act a law. And without his leadership, the opposition would ensure that the bill would disappear, buried in a Senate committee.

• • •

JOHNSON WAS FORLORN. "MY political garments have been divided," he moaned, "and upon my vesture do they intend to cast lots." He was convinced he had no political future. Now that he was out of office, homesteading would no longer be a part of Washington's legislative agenda.

Johnson's melancholy, however, was short-lived. He made up his mind that he would eventually return to Washington. But first, in his practical, determined way, he reinvented himself. If he could no longer be a congressman, he would become governor.

It was a tough, no-holds-barred race, yet in 1853 he was sworn in as Tennessee's governor. When he ran again in 1855, it was another battle. He won that election, too. And Johnson used his victory to push through significant legislation. Tennessee's first public school system and the state's first library were created during his governorship.

While serving as governor, Johnson's commitment to the egalitarian belief that every man deserved his own home never flagged. It was always on his mind, in his heart. When he returned to Washington in 1857 after his election to the U.S. Senate, Johnson was eager to introduce a new homesteading bill.

It was a tense, partisan time in the country, and Washington was no less divided. The Civil War loomed, and every issue was filtered through a North-South, proslavery, antislavery mind-set. Homesteading was no exception. Johnson's fellow southerners were now vehemently opposed to giving away free land. They dismissed it as one more nefarious scheme to make slaves free men by offering them farms. The northerners, though, were growing more sympathetic. Some were even as effusive as Johnson in their newfound support. "If a man has a right on earth," Representative Galusha A. Grow of Pennsylvania proclaimed on the floor of the House, "he has a right to land enough to rear a habitation on."

Despite the deepening polarization in Congress and the uncertainties facing the Union, with a true believer's single-mindedness Johnson remained focused on his agenda. He brought a new homestead bill before the Senate in December 1857.

His proposal mirrored the bill that had previously passed in the House: heads of families would receive 160 acres provided that they reside on and cultivate the land for a set period. But Johnson found that the mood of the lawmakers had changed.

With war increasingly imminent, too many northern senators feared that it was the wrong time to deplete the national Treasury by giving away land for free. The southerners for their part predicted that in the aftermath of the U.S. Supreme Court's decision in the *Dred Scott* case sanctioning slavery in the territories, slaves in these remote areas would take ownership of 160 acres and declare themselves free. The bill was doomed in the Senate even as it was introduced. Quite quickly, senators buried it by voting to delay consideration until the next session.

Two years later, though, during the brief winter session of 1859, the House once more passed a Homestead Act. It was not as generous as Johnson's original bill, but the years of struggle had taught him to be pragmatic. He ignored the bill's shortcomings, and championed it in the Senate. This time the vote was close. Vice President John Cabell Breckinridge, as president of the Senate, was called on to break the tie. He voted along with the southern members, and the bill was once again tabled.

Johnson refused to let the issue die. He fully realized that he did not have the support of the chairman of the Committee on Public Lands. He understood that without the chairman's endorsement, a bill could never be passed. Yet he also was determined to keep homesteading as part of the congressional dialogue. He reintroduced the act in December.

Three months later, in March 1860, the House passed its own homesteading bill. It provided land grants with few restrictions to settlers, and it was a bill that Johnson, in his heart, felt was both generous and democratic. It was also legislation that Johnson knew could never become law.

Johnson's years of high-minded battles ending inevitably in stunning defeats had taught him that the path to victory was measured out in compromises. The House bill was too liberal to succeed in the southern-dominated Senate. So Johnson tried to tailor it to fit his colleagues' prejudices and concerns. He reached out to his fellow southerners with a proposal to limit eligibility to those heads of families who would pay 12 cents per acre. But even this was too generous for many of the senators.

Obligingly, Johnson crafted a more restrictive bill. It included many of the terms favored by the Committee on Public Lands. For example, the land offered to settlers was only to be tracts that had previously been for sale but had not attracted buyers, and the price per acre would be more than doubled, to 25 cents. Also, immigrants who had filed for citizenship would be eligible for land ownership.

Johnson was once again attacked, this time not only by homesteading opponents but also by supporters. They charged that this compromise was not a true free land act. Johnson, they bellowed, had betrayed the cause. But while the personal criticisms left him feeling wounded, with an impressive practicality, Johnson refused to back down. He stuck by the legislation and fought for its passage.

On May 10, 1860, the Senate passed the Homestead Act. It had been a fourteen-year battle. The bill that passed was a carefully crafted compromise that bore only few similarities to the liberal proposals Johnson had originally championed. There were many restrictions on who could receive land grants and the per acre costs far exceeded those in previous bills. But for the first time both chambers of Congress had passed homesteading legislation. Now the bills could move on to conference committee.

There were three conference sessions, more heated negotiations, and, ultimately, more compromises. To appease southern lawmakers, Johnson glumly agreed that the right to buy land could not be offered to *all* males over age twenty-one, but only to heads of households—a provision that tacitly precluded slaves. To placate the Senate further, the House's version, which included all unsurveyed federal tracts, was now limited to only half of the public lands that had not yet been surveyed. While to get support in the House, the conference agreed to omit a requirement that land be marketable within two years. With these modifications, a patchwork Homestead Bill was finally passed.

President Buchanan was the last hurdle. He decided that the proposed law would be "the ax at the root of our present admirable land system." On June 22, 1860, he vetoed the bill. There was a move to try to override the presidential veto, but even Johnson voted against it. He thought it made more strategic sense to call for reconsideration of the law. This, too, met with little support. The Homestead Act was now dead.

And apparently deeply buried. The nation was consumed by more pressing concerns. The future of the Union was in jeopardy, and a homesteading bill now seemed unimportant, an irrelevancy. It was legislation—and perhaps even an idea—whose time in the national consciousness had passed.

But when Abraham Lincoln was elected president in 1860, he brought to the office a commitment to homesteading. He had campaigned in support of the issue, and now that he was in power he was determined to make free land for settlers a national right. With the secession of the southern states, the most vocal congressional opposition had been eliminated. When a new bill was introduced, it passed in the House in February 1862 by an overwhelming vote of 106 to 16. Three months later it won Senate approval, by another substantial majority, 33 to 7. With a triumphant Andrew Johnson in attendance, President Lincoln on May 20, 1862, signed the Homestead Act into law.

Come along, come along, don't be alarmed;
Uncle Sam is rich enough to give us all a farm!

So went a popular camp song of the 1870s, and many settlers gleefully sang the lyrics and endorsed the sentiment as they headed west for new homes. Dan Freeman made the first claim for farmland in Beatrice, Montana, under the Homestead Act on January 1, 1863. Over the next 123 years that the law (and subsequent modifications) remained in effect, more than 2 million individuals would file claims. Two hundred and seventy million western acres—about 11 percent of today's America—would be settled by pioneers who received homestead land grants. The seeds of American prosperity—the nation's future wealth, creativity, and power—would be planted by the families who used the Homestead Act to help shape their own futures.

Yet for all the program's successes, for all the ambitious, even noble ideals that motivated Johnson and the original proponents, the failures also are striking. The overpopulation in the East was never alleviated. For every settler who staked a claim, another simply looked at the available land and walked off in dismay. Only about 783,000 farmers—less than half of all those who had filed claims—stayed on their land long enough to receive deeds.

One problem was that arid conditions made the western lands much more difficult to farm and inhabit than pioneers had imagined. Another was that the land in the Great Plains, where much of the homesteading took place, was more appropriate for cattle ranches and mining; these sorts of enterprises required more than 160 acres and were certainly too expensive for down-at-their-heels settlers. But in the end, this dismal record was not so much evidence of a lack of American will as it was proof of the widespread corruption and legal abuses that undermined the potential of the Homestead Act.

The best land in most locales, for example, was never made available to the settlers. The Pacific Railway acts of 1862 and 1864 gave the railroads generous grants of land adjacent to their tracks and the companies often would pick routes that would maximize their receiving the richest acres. Since lawmakers never knew the precise location of the proposed routes, enormous tracts of farmable land would need to be withheld. To complicate matters further, the Railroad Act also stated that no land could be settled within 80 acres of a railroad grant. All many of the forlorn pioneers could do was claim isolated and unattractive tracts, land far from public transportation or civilization. A flurry of similarly restrictive federal laws—the 1873 Timber Culture Act; the 1877 Desert Land Act; the 1878 Timber and Stone Act—also worked to limit the public land available to settlers.

Then, to make a daunting situation nearly hopeless, unscrupulous lawmakers began to write loopholes into the act. The "commutation clause" was one such amendment. It drastically altered the law by allowing settlers to buy their land at $1.25 per acre after only six months of occupation. Therefore, after a brief occupancy, the so-called settlers would sell their tracts to monopolists or speculators who rountinely swept in with offers.

The government's General Land Office condemned this practice. "Commutation is the clause in the Homestead law," it noted in a strongly admonitory report, "under which citizens who are not farmers or ranchers, and who have no intention of ever becoming such, enter agricultural lands. . . . Not one in a hundred is ever occupied as a home after the commutation," the report continued. Instead, the tracts became "part of some large timber holding or a parcel of a cattle or sheep ranch." Yet, for all the General Land Office's anger, it was powerless to stop the practice.

In the meantime, inventive settlers had discovered another

loophole that allowed them to work with speculators to circumvent even further the spirit of the Homestead Act. Under the Pre-Emption Law, settlers could buy up to 160 acres of land on which they lived before it was put up for public sale. New legislation allowed that purchases under the Pre-Emption Law and the Homestead Act could be combined. Therefore, it was possible to acquire 320 acres at the bargain price of $1.25 an acre. Equally providential, other laws permitted more land to be inexpensively bundled into these tracts. Under the Timber Culture Act of 1873, for example, an owner could increase the size of his property by an additional 160 acres if he planted and cultivated at least 40 acres of trees over the next decade—and, perhaps most alluring of all, the owner did not even need to live on such a property.

This myriad of laws added up to a profitable mathematics for speculators. By combining tracts acquired under the different statutes, a single individual could amass a vast fiefdom—all at bargain prices subsidized by the federal government, and all made available by a government motivated by the lofty ideal of westward expansion. Huge private estates developed. William Chapman ruled 650,000 acres of California territory; Ezra Cornell controlled 500,000 acres of Wisconsin pinelands.

So much for ideals. The Homestead Act had been designed to help impoverished city dwellers and hardscrabble farmers. But in the end, the largest group of beneficiaries were the speculators, the railroads, and a cabal of unscrupulous politicians. A beleaguered Congress did an accounting and was forced to acknowledge that of the billion acres owned by the government, only one acre in five went to small farmers.

• • •

CHANGES IN THE LAW, many lawmakers realized, had to be made. But galvanizing Congress to pass legislation that would tighten the loopholes was an ambitious, perhaps wishful task. After all, many of those who profited most spectacularly from the Homestead Act and the other land grant bills were the same wealthy and influential individuals whose support and dollars the politicians counted on to win elections.

Nevertheless, the abuses were so egregious that Congress was motivated to act. With the Southern Homestead Act of 1866, legislators took a first step toward rectifying matters. This bill stipulated that all public lands in Arkansas, Alabama, Florida, Louisiana, and Mississippi were prohibited from sale. They would be distributed in 80-acre parcels—an allotment that was later doubled—under the new Homestead Bill. Therefore, an additional 46 million acres was made available to settlers.

Other reforms followed. In 1871, Congress repealed the overly generous railroad land grants. In 1889, the selling of public land at auction was eliminated; these tracts, too, would be available to homesteaders. In 1890, a law was at last passed limiting the amount of land an individual could legally bundle to 320 acres. A year later, suddenly zealous lawmakers rewrote the language of the commutation clause to prevent abuses, and, more dramatic, voted to repeal the Pre-Emption Law.

But while these new acts prevented speculators from carving out large dominions assembled from cheap government land, there remained another problem that the lawmakers needed to address. The Homestead Act had failed to alleviate the eastern labor crisis.

For the urban poor, it simply cost too much to make the move westward. Cross-country travel was expensive. The price of equipment needed to start and sustain a farm was prohibitive. And since it generally took several harvests before a farm could earn a profit, the prospect of relying on savings for support and sustenance was an impossibility for city dwellers who had none. The promise of "free" western land was simply pie-in-the-sky—"To the common laborer," the historian Fred A. Shannon wrote, "as futile as a signboard pointing to the end of a rainbow."

YET EVEN WHILE POLITICAL mischief and corruption worked against the program and tarnished the realization of its egalitarian vision, it is still important to recognize—and celebrate—what the Homestead Act accomplished. It did nothing less than to help to build America:

Between 1850 and 1920, the number of the nation's farms quadrupled—and a significant majority of these began on what was once public lands.

Waves of new immigrants, people with skill, ambition, and creativity, flocked to the country—many enticed by the glittering promise of the West.

Important precedents in federal subsidies were established—public dollars could be benevolently invested with the realistic return of creating self-sufficient communities.

It was the largest transfer of public land to private ownership in history; a total of almost 300 million acres were settled by homesteaders between 1862 and 1955—and in the process, civilization and stability rooted in the western and northern half of the western hemisphere.

Andrew Johnson's steadfast commitment demonstrated once again that one man with vision and persistence can mobilize a reluctant government to act boldly and spend wisely. And in the end, this investment can work to enrich the entire nation.

The Panama Canal

A T 9:40 ON THE night of February 15, 1898, as the USS *Maine* was anchored in Havana Harbor, a booming explosion suddenly rocked the battleship. Darting flames ignited the five tons of powder stored for the vessel's big guns and this new blast was catastrophic. The forward section of the *Maine* was obliterated. Burning oil and fiery wreckage streaked the night sky with a hellish illumination, and what remained of the nearly 7,000-ton warship sank rapidly. Two hundred and sixty-six sailors died that night, and another eight later succumbed to their injuries.

The cause of the initial explosion was never conclusively determined, but for many Americans there was no need for any investigation. "Remember the *Maine*, to hell with Spain!" became a battle cry. And with tensions bristling between the United States and Spain, as a war in Cuba grew increasingly imminent, it became a strategic necessity to position another battleship off the Cuban coast.

The USS *Oregon* was one of the new fleet of long-range cruising battleships. Championed by Assistant Secretary of the Navy Theodore Roosevelt, these mighty warships were built so that America could stand up with power and defiance to the European imperial nations. "Speak softly and carry a big stick," Roosevelt had preached. On March 12, 1898, the *Oregon*—one of the nation's biggest sticks—was ordered to Cuba.

Only the *Oregon* was stationed on the Pacific Coast, in waters off San Francisco. As the country moved closer to war, the battleship began a 14,700-mile race around South America, through the stormy Straits of Magellan, and on toward Cuba.

It was a dangerous, nonstop voyage and its progress was avidly followed by an anxious American public—including, most consequentially as history would prove, Teddy Roosevelt. Roosevelt was no longer the assistant secretary of the Navy. He had resigned to become a lieutenant colonel in the Cuba-bound "Rough Riders" cavalry unit. As Roosevelt read the press reports charting the battleship's journey, he was now a front-line officer counting on supporting fire from the *Oregon*'s powerful batteries.

Despite the captain's determined efforts, the voyage took sixty-seven days. The warship arrived off Santiago, Cuba, nearly two months after the outbreak of the Spanish-American War. And a frustrated Colonel Roosevelt had realized firsthand, as he would later explain, that if the United States were to become a world power, if the country were to be able to defend itself and engage enemies on both coasts, then an isthmian canal, a shortcut linking the Atlantic and the Pacific oceans, would have to be built.

In 1901, when Roosevelt, following the assassination of William McKinley, became president, he was prepared to act on the lesson he had learned while serving in the Spanish-American War. "If we are to hold our own in the struggle for naval and commercial supremacy," he told the nation with almost evangelical fervor, "we must build up our power without our borders. . . . We must build the isthmian canal, and we must grasp the points of vantage which will enable us to have our say in deciding the destiny of the oceans of the east and the west."

The story of how a steely President Theodore Roosevelt successfully mobilized a reluctant Congress and nation to build the Panama Canal is another case study of farsighted and tenacious leadership. It is an example of how a large and daring investment of federal funds beyond the country's borders—the first in U.S. history—can create an infrastructure that will bring long-term commercial and strategic benefits to the nation.

Yet at the same time, Roosevelt's construction of the Panama Canal is also an imperialistic saga. It is a cautionary tale of a ruthlessly pragmatic foreign policy that set out to expand America's global influence regardless of the rights of other sovereign nations. And the legacies of Roosevelt's power politics, a pattern of international bullying and blatantly unconstitutional actions, are blemishes on the national character that continue to affect the country, too.

• • •

THE STRATEGIC AND GEOGRAPHICAL importance of the Panamanian isthmus first became apparent to the self-interested world powers in the sixteenth century. Connecting North and South America, this narrow strip of land with its low mountains and navigable rivers had been claimed for the king of Spain in 1513 by the explorer Vasco Núñez de Balboa. Very quickly the isthmus became a well-trafficked trade route. For two hundred years, the Spanish Empire transported rich cargoes of gold and silver from Peru via pack trains and riverboats that traversed Panama. And from the first decades of Spanish control, a prescient Charles I (1516–56) had considered the construction of a canal across the isthmus to accelerate passage between the Atlantic and Pacific Oceans. But before the plan could progress, the Spanish Empire began to collapse.

In 1821, as an overextended Spain was busily trying to defend its many colonies, Panama took advantage of the unsettled situation and declared its independence. This newfound sovereignty, however, was short-lived. The nation was quickly annexed by Colombia.

Yet even as Colombia tightened its control over a resentful Panama, France also fixed an acquisitive eye on the isthmus. At an International Congress on navigation held in Paris, Count Ferdinand de Lesseps announced to the world his country's interest in building an interoceanic canal through Panama.

De Lesseps was the perfect spokesman for France. He came from a prominent family and was smart, well-read, and extremely personable. But most significant, he was a national hero, the man who despite lack of formal training or in-depth engineering know-how had designed the Suez Canal and made it a reality.

In 1876, La Société Civile Internationale du Interocéanique de Darien was formed to study the feasibility of possible sites for a canal in Panama. Neither a stockholder nor an officer in the company, de Lesseps held only the vague title of head of the society's Committee of Initiative. Nevertheless, the autocratic count single-handedly made all the group's important decisions.

It was de Lesseps who chose the two French naval lieutenants, Lucien N. B. Wyse and Armand Reclus, and then sent them off to Panama. Their mission: to find the best site for a canal allowing a direct passage between the Pacific Ocean and the Caribbean Sea, the gateway to the Atlantic. When the two lieutenants returned, de Lesseps carefully studied the potential routes they had suggested; and then, full of a booming frustration, dismissed them all. Instead, the count ordered the two naval officers back to Panama. Their instructions were to survey options that would be more to his liking.

Wyse and Reclus returned to Paris this time with two proposals. One was a plan for a sea-level canal. This route would require a 7,700-meter tunnel, but this didn't daunt the confident de Lesseps. He grew convinced that this sea-level canal was the best route and could be constructed with relative ease. The count once again dispatched Wyse to the region, only this time the naval officer had a new mission. He was to negotiate a treaty with Colombia that would give France's Société Civile the exclusive rights to build a canal in Panama.

At the same time, de Lesseps also realized that France—and the Société Civile—would need international, political, financial, and perhaps even scientific support for such a bold, costly, and technically innovative undertaking. In May 1879, with de Lesseps working feverishly behind the scenes to orchestrate the event, an International Congress for the Study of an Interoceanic Canal was convened. In de Lesseps's mind, this Congress would simply be a celebratory gathering. It would give a quick and enthusiastic endorsement to his plan.

De Lesseps had been naive. Fourteen new canal proposals were presented as challenges to his selected route. Including, to the count's great astonishment, a radical alternative offered up by the two upstart American delegates.

DURING THE NINETEENTH CENTURY, America was forging its way to becoming a world power. The Louisiana Purchase (1803), the explorations of Lewis and Clark (1804–06), the settlement of Oregon, the Mexican War (1846–48) and the subsequent acquisitions of California and New Mexico—all these developments helped to transform the young republic into a newly rich nation that stretched across the continent from the Atlantic to the Pacific.

And as America grew, the nation began to consider the new challenges that came with its expanded borders. Its Navy now had to defend two coastlines 3,000 miles apart. No less vital or daunting, goods and people needed to move quickly and safely across the continent from one seaboard to another.

The completion of the transcontinental railroad offered one way for merchandise and travelers to get across the country. The sailing route around Cape Horn provided another alternative. But the discovery of gold in California sent unprecedented hordes flocking to the west coast, and both these routes were overwhelmed by passengers. Suddenly, there was a new urgent demand for cross-country travel, and the nation began to consider other swift routes to unite the continent. Among many proposals, the possibility of a direct nautical journey via a canal cutting across Panama received a great deal of attention in the press and in Congress.

The outbreak of the Civil War, however, forced the nation to confront more immediate priorities. When the war ended, lawmakers once again began to focus on the construction of a canal. Negotiations with Panama produced two treaties that would allow the United States to build a canal across the isthmus. Both treaties, though, were ultimately rejected by senators reluctant to authorize large sums for a project that would be built beyond America's borders.

Nevertheless, the Grant administration refused to allow the possibility of a canal to die. Between 1870 and 1875, it enthusiastically funded surveys by the Interoceanic Canal Commission to plot a variety of canal routes.

In the winter of 1875, after reviewing all the proposals, the commission recommended a route through Nicaragua. This would be, the commission decided, less costly than a Panamanian canal and would present fewer engineering problems.

It was this carefully considered plan for a Nicaraguan canal that, to de Lesseps's surprise and sudden concern, the U.S. representatives presented at the 1879 International Congress.

THE AMERICANS AT THE congress did not offer the only viable challenge to the sea-level canal. To de Lesseps's further consternation, another Frenchman, Adolphe de Lepinay, created a stir with a forceful presentation of a plan for building a Panamanian canal, but one with an innovative lock system. De Lepinay, who had worked in the region while building the rail line connecting Córdoba to Veracruz, focused on overcoming what his experience had convinced him were inherent dangers in the de Lesseps route. He predicted that in the rainy season, Panama's Charges River would overflow and swamp the sea-level canal route. To avoid this, he proposed damming both the Charges and the Rio Grande rivers and creating two lakes that would accommodate the inevitably rising rainy season waters. By managing the Charges River, de Lepinay argued, his design would take less time to build, require less capital, and very likely result in few fatalities and accidents during construction.

It was a proposal that was both ingenious and compelling. Along with the well-received plan from the two Americans, it, too, threatened to change the mood of the conference. A panicked de Lesseps rushed into action.

The count quickly called for a general session of the International Congress and he used this assembly to present his proposition. It was a masterful performance—detailed, persuasive, and brimming with confident predictions. The Technical Committee overwhelmingly recommended de Lesseps's sea-level route by a margin of 74–8, with thirty-eight delegates abstaining.

A furious President Rutherford Hayes, invoking the Monroe Doctrine, responded to the International Congress's support for the French plan with a succinct warning. "The policy of this country is a canal under American control," the president sternly announced.

But de Lesseps paid little attention to this warning. He was determined to build his canal.

CONSTRUCTION BEGAN IN 1881, and from the start, it was a troubled project. The French had breezily begun work in Panama believing that the obstacles they'd face would be similar to those in building the Suez Canal, and that these problems could also be swiftly overcome. They were wrong. Their plans needed to be radically revised to deal with the unique engineering obstacles that existed on the isthmus, and the failure to make these preliminary adjustments created structural errors and crippling cost overruns. But even more shortsighted, the cavalier French did not anticipate the grave health problems they would encounter in Panama.

As with Napoléon's troops in Saint-Dominigue, yellow fever and malaria attacked canal construction workers. There was no known medical regimen to control the disease, and thousands began to die. There were no safe havens; even the hospitals were breeding grounds. The plague was devastating.

After losing 20,000 men and spending 1.435 billion francs ($287 million; a colossal sum at the time), with no way to prevent the loss of more lives or the escalating expenditures, a beleaguered de Lesseps ordered work to stop. In February 1889, after eight demanding years of construction had excavated 50 billion cubic feet of earth and rock, the Compagnie Universelle du Canal Interocéanique was liquidated. More than 800,000 shareholders faced the impending loss of a substantial portion of their investments.

Yet there were still many in France who were not willing to abandon the project. With the original Wyse Concession with Colombia set to expire in 1893, an ambitious new entity, the Compagnie Nouvelle du Canal de Panama, brokered a ten-year extension.

Despite the company's high hopes, however, it could not persuade investors to put up the capital necessary for the project. After struggling without any success for several years, the members of the Compagnie Nouvelle were faced with a demoralizing yet necessary decision: they could abandon the project entirely, or they could attempt to sell off what they still controlled. Compagnie Nouvelle's collapse marked the end of France's efforts to build and operate a Panamanian canal.

AS FRANCE'S INTEREST IN a canal died, America's was rekindled. A succession of events had forced an ambitious nation to reconsider the need for a canal.

First, in 1897, President William McKinley signed a treaty making Hawaii a U.S. territory. This acquisition reinforced the necessity of a naval presence in both the Atlantic and the Pacific— and the strategic requirement of a quick navigable route that would allow warships to rush to either coast in times of crisis.

A year later, the Spanish-American War broke out. With the nation anxiously following its progress, as has been detailed, the USS *Oregon* needed to race around Cape Horn to the Caribbean Sea. Had the Panama Canal existed, it would have shortened the battleship's voyage by a crucial three weeks.

Finally, under the terms of the Treaty of Paris that ended the Spanish-American War, Spain sold the Philippines to the United States for $20 million. This acquisition also increased the need for a swifter, more direct trade route from the Atlantic Coast to the Pacific. While the growing Filipino resistance to foreign control—Spain had brazenly sold the islands despite their having declared their independence in June 1898—raised the likelihood that American warships would often need to be speedily dispatched to the region.

As a result of these developments, President McKinley called for a second Walker Commission to reconsider plans for building an isthmian passage. The commission dutifully surveyed routes through Nicaragua, Panama, and the isthmus of Darien. In the end, it recommended the Nicaraguan route.

A bill was quickly introduced in Congress to support the building of a canal in Nicaragua. There was, however, a diplomatic problem. In 1850, the United States had signed the Clayton-Bulwer Treaty with Britain. This agreement specified that the two nations would not only cooperate to build an isthmian canal, but also that neither would proceed independently of the other. And Britain had firmly announced that it was dead-set against the Nicaraguan route.

An international crisis was averted when a persistent U.S. Secretary of State John Hay persuaded Lord Paunceforte, the British ambassador, to enter into new negotiations. After many spirited and intransigent discussions, the two diplomats ultimately settled on an agreement that superseded the 1850 treaty and allowed American fortification of the Nicaraguan canal.

Construction of the Nicaraguan project now seemed inevitable. But then on September 6, 1901, President McKinley was shot twice as he greeted visitors to the Pan-American Exposition in Buffalo, New York, and he died eight days later.

Theodore Roosevelt became president. His experiences on the front lines in the Spanish-American War as well as his reading of Captain Alfred Thayer Mahan's book, *The Influence of Sea Power Upon History* (1890), had convinced him that seapower would make America into a world power. But the U.S. Navy's ability to control and police both the Atlantic and Pacific would only be possible if there was a canal linking the two oceans. A canal was a strategic necessity if America was to achieve, as Roosevelt fervently believed, its God-given international destiny. Constructing a canal, he insisted, was a national imperative. He just had one problem with the pending project: Roosevelt, a man of iron will, wanted to build the canal in Panama, not Nicaragua.

ONLY IT WAS APPARENTLY too late. To the new president's dismay, the Hepburn Bill in support of the Nicaraguan site was already being pushed through the House of Representatives. On January 7, 1902, just days after the lawmakers had returned from their Christmas recess, the bill was quickly approved, only 2 votes shy of unanimous support. Senator Tyler Morgan, a powerful southerner who served as chairman of the Senate Committee on Interoceanic Canals and a staunch supporter of the Nicaraguan route, swiftly introduced the bill in the Senate. Approval seemed a certainty.

But before the Senate could consider the bill, unforeseen events happened in France. And a cunning Roosevelt moved with alacrity to take advantage of these new circumstances.

The president of the Compagnie Nouvelle had abruptly resigned, and the panicked stockholders had met in Paris with the small hope of salvaging what they could from an increasingly desperate situation. Previously, the company had demanded $109 million for its Panamanian holdings. Now it dramatically reduced the asking price of these assets to a bargain amount—$40 million.

When Roosevelt heard the news, he realized this was the opportunity he had been hoping for. He convened a closed-door meeting of the Walker Commission. In a display of executive power that was more dictatorial than presidential, Roosevelt announced to the stunned committee members his unilateral decisions to accept the Compagnie Nouvelle's $40 million offer and, regardless of the passage of the Hepburn Bill, to build the canal in Panama. For the sake of the nation, he imperiously demanded that the commission members rescind their support for a Nicaraguan canal and instead unanimously choose the Panama site. Cowered by the unflinching Roosevelt, the commission agreed. In January 1902, a triumphant president submitted this new report to Congress.

The new president's single-minded commitment to the Panama site soon gained tactical support in the Senate. As the Hepburn Bill was being debated, Senator John Spooner introduced an amendment that had been carefully designed to bolster Roosevelt's intentions. It specified that the United States would purchase the French holdings in Panama if (1) the cost did not exceed $40 million; and (2) a treaty with Colombia could be negotiated within "a reasonable time." If these provisions could not be fulfilled, then—and only then—would the president seek an agreement for a route through Nicaragua.

The amendment was entered into debate before the Committee on Interoceanic Canals in early February, and now nature seemed to conspire to promote the Panamanian site. As the discussions began in Washington, a volcano erupted on the Caribbean island of Martinique. The loss of life was devastating. Supporters of the amendment ominously pointed out there was not one but fourteen volcanoes in Nicaragua. (That many were extinct seemed to be irrelevant.) What would happen to a canal, to America's investment, if a volcano exploded, spewing molten lava over Nicaragua? they worried. But Senator Morgan, the committee chairman, called in many favors and kept his supporters in line. On March 10, the committee voted to support the Nicaraguan route.

The bill now moved on to the entire Senate, and from the start of the debate the battle lines were firmly drawn. Senator Morgan once again led the support for the Nicaragua site, and proceeded to dismiss the tragedy in Martinique as an unfortunate but rare occurrence. The pro-Panama contingent was led by the powerful Senator Mark Hanna, the well-connected chairman of the Republican Party. Hanna was a skilled orator and he delivered a well-reasoned speech on the Senate floor citing favorable engineering reports and capital projections. Still, a majority of the senators appeared ready to support the Nicaraguan route.

But days before the vote, every senator received a present from a French engineer, Philippe-Jean Bunau-Varilla, who had worked with de Lesseps and who now aligned himself with Hanna. It was not an expensive gift; in fact, its intrinsic value was only a few cents. Yet it turned the vote around. It was a Nicaraguan postage stamp with an image of an erupting volcano. The prospect of a volcano spewing lava over the canal, of a multimillion-dollar investment suddenly destroyed, now seemed a distinct possibility. A disaster similar to the one in Martinique seemed likely, perhaps commonplace, in Nicaragua. After all, even the country's postage stamps acknowledged the ferocity of its erupting volcanoes.

On June 19, 2008, the Senate voted in favor of the Panama canal route. A week later, the House approved the bill. And a jubilant President Roosevelt did not hesitate to sign the bill into law. America could now build its canal.

OR COULD IT?

In all the congressional debate over the canal, very little attention had been paid to one very large and encumbering legal reality: the province of Panama was governed by Colombia. The United States had to receive Colombia's approval and consent before it could build in its territory.

Negotiations now began between America and Colombia. It did not take long for mutual frustrations and resentments to boil over into hot anger. The Colombian government had recently come to power in a coup and was determined to prove it could not be intimidated. Its chief negotiator was José Vicente Concha, a former minister of war, who spoke no English and had to consult with the Colombian president before he could comment on even the most routine matters. America's lead diplomat was John Hay, the secretary of state. A veteran negotiator, a man of aristocratic breeding and steady temperament, nevertheless even Hay was undone by the adamancy and recalcitrance of the Colombians. He was trapped, he would say, in "the most thankless and exasperating episode in a long career."

Roosevelt's patience quickly wore thin. American power, he

decided without any qualms, would accomplish what diplomacy could not. He would shake a "big stick," and the frightened Colombians would have no choice but to acquiesce. On September 16, 1902, the USS *Cincinnati* anchored in Panama's Colón Harbor, and American forces took control of the Panama railway and occupied Panama City. After three tense months, Colombia agreed to appoint a new negotiator to lead the canal discussions with the United States.

Dr. Tomás Herrán was a graduate of Georgetown University and, to the delight of the American contingent, spoke fluent English. As his counterpart, Hay chose an influential lawyer who had openly support Hanna's pro-Panama efforts in the Senate, William Nelson Cromwell. With the selection of these two new diplomats and the lingering presence of the *Cincinnati* in Colón, the negotiations moved forward.

On January 23, 1903, the Hay-Herrán Treaty was signed. Colombia would receive a modest $10 million payment from the United States for the entire Canal Zone and an additional $250,000 yearly annuity. The U.S. Senate, over the objections of the still vocal Nicaraguan lobby, ratified the treaty in mid-March.

At last, America could begin construction on its Panamanian canal. But before the excavations started, the unexpected happened. On August 12, a defiant Colombian Senate unanimously rejected the Hay-Herrán Treaty.

ROOSEVELT WAS FURIOUS. IT seemed incredible to him that the Colombians dared to interfere with American destiny. "Those contemptible little creatures in Bogotá ought to understand how much they are jeopardizing things and imperiling their own future," he ranted. The president decided to send troops to Panama to take control of the country.

As Roosevelt was finalizing his brazen plan for military intervention, the State Department was pursuing a more covert strategy. This scheme involved instigating a revolution that would result in Panama's seceding from Colombia's grasp. Two employees of the Panama Railroad and Steamship Company, Dr. Manuel Amador Guerro and José Agustín Arango, were selected to be the titular leaders of the revolution. But when Guerro arrived in Washington to hammer out the specific details of American support, he was unsuccessful in even arranging meetings with Cromwell or Hay. He did succeed, though, in talking with Bunau-Varilla, the Frenchman whose inspired postage stamp caper had turned the Senate vote around. And as things worked out, Bunau-Varilla was the only advocate the fledgling revolutionary needed.

Bunau-Varilla met with both President Roosevelt and Secretary of State Hay and made a succinct, practical, and entirely unconstitutional case for an American role in a Panamanian uprising. If there was a revolution, he pointed out, America would be seen by the world not as a bully but as the liberator of an oppressed people. The Panamanians would simply declare their independence, and when Colombian tried to quell the revolt, the U.S. forces would land to protect the rights of the besieged Panamanians. The Colombian troops would present no problem, Bunau-Varilla assured the Americans. Guerro, in fact, had convinced him that with a mere $100,000 payoff, the Colombian troops would quickly withdraw from Panama. This was far less, the Frenchman pointed out, than the estimated $6 million that would be required to finance a "traditional" and no doubt bloody military revolution.

On November 3, the USS *Nashville* arrived in Colón. That same day, Panama declared its independence. As American forces took strategic positions throughout the country, the Colombian troops began to withdraw from the isthmus. A mere three days after the "spontaneous" revolution, on November 6, the United States officially recognized the nation of Panama.

With similar speed, the United States and Panama negotiated and signed the Hay-Bunau-Varilla Treaty. Under the agreement, the new government of Panama received a $10 million payment and a $250,000 annuity, the identical terms that the Colombian Senate had rejected. And in return, Panama increased the six-mile-wide Canal Zone to ten miles, authorized Compagnie Nouvelle to transfer its assets to the United States (for the previously agreed $40 million payment), and granted the United States sovereignty in the Canal Zone in perpetuity.

It was a shrewd, opportunistic deal for America. The young nation of Panama had given away an extremely valuable asset and had blithely accepted only a small payment in return. Yet the bigger loser was Colombia. In the aftermath of its rejection of the Hay-Herrán Treaty, the country watched helplessly as a vindictive and powerful America engineered the plot to sever the entire province of Panama from its control.

On February 23, 1904, the United States ratified the treaty with Panama. Roosevelt could finally build his canal.

• • •

MANY AMERICANS, THOUGH, WERE astounded and disturbed by what had been done to secure the rights to build the Panamanian canal. The cost had been, they complained, prohibitive. The $10 million paid to Panama in addition to the $40 million the Compagnie Nouvelle received—a total of $50 million!—was more than any territorial acquisition in U.S. history. The price of the entire Louisiana Territory had been only $15 million; Alaska had been bought for $7.2 million; and the Philippines had cost just $20 million. Further, this $50 million payout—a staggering sum in turn-of-the-century dollars—was just the initial expenditure. Untold tens of millions of additional dollars would be needed once the actual construction of the canal began.

No less disturbing to many of the critics of transaction was the ruthless conduct of the United States. America, the canal's opponents charged, had behaved with cold-blooded self-interest. Such amoral imperialistic behavior violated the democratic spirit on which the nation had been founded. The country's actions in Panama were not simply wrong but illegal, violations of both international law and the U.S. Constitution.

Joseph Pulitzer's *New York World* fueled the opposition campaign, and adamantly hammered away at the president. The paper's articles and editorials throughout 1908 charged that Roosevelt had unscrupulously instigated the revolution in Panama to protect the French investments of his friends, particularly Cromwell and Bunau-Varilla. Full of self-righteous fury, Roosevelt sued Pulitzer for libel.

But even as the president publicly raged, he also methodically focused on building the canal. He created an Isthmian Canal Commission to oversee the project, completed the official transfer of the Compagnie Nouvelle holdings to the United States, and appointed a military officer, Major General George W. Davis, as the first governor of the Canal Zone.

In a small ceremony under a broiling Panamanian sun on May 4, 1904, the French handed over the keys to the storehouses and one hospital to Major General Davis. The Canal Zone was now under American control.

There was little excitement, little sense of anticipation, that hot afternoon. Instead, the mood was grim. The jungle had grown wild, reclaiming the few structures the French had left behind. Squads of engineers and construction workers were needed. Housing and sanitation for the anticipated work crews was nearly non-existent. Construction equipment still had not been shipped. And, arguably the greatest reason for despair, there was no medical plan for treating the inevitable outbreaks of malaria and yellow fever. America could begin to build its canal, but now the reality of the challenge was suddenly daunting.

YET THE AMERICANS WENT to work. As the first contingents of construction workers arrived, so did Dr. William Crawford Gorgas. Gorgas had assisted Dr. Walter Reed in his groundbreaking study of yellow fever in Cuba, and as the project's chief sanitary officer he had come to Panama with a precautionary medical strategy. Central to Gorgas's plan was the realization that with as many as 34,000 workers in the Canal Zone, the facilities of a small city would be needed—and that this infrastructure of housing, sanitation, and mess halls had to be built and then rigorously maintained with the specific intention of preventing disease.

Gorgas offered a series of prudent, prophylactic proposals aimed at preventing the outbreaks of yellow fever and malaria that had decimated the French workers. John F. Wallace, the project's chief engineer, dismissed these precautions as unnecessary and too expensive. Soon, inevitably, malaria began to gallop through the workforce.

Fortunately, before the plague could escalate, a new chief engineer arrived. John Stevens swiftly appraised the situation, overruled Wallace, and gave Gorgas resources and a free hand in making precautionary medical decisions. By November 1905, yellow fever had been eradicated in the isthmus.

Yet even as workers continued to arrive, even as shiploads of heavy construction equipment were unloaded daily, there remained one central problem before work on the canal could move beyond the relatively straightforward task of excavation: What kind of canal should be built? A lock canal or a sea-level canal?

Stevens had arrived in Panama convinced that the sea-level approach, the same solution advocated by de Lesseps, made the most engineering sense. But after his firsthand inspection of the isthmus, he changed his mind. He grew convinced that one large reason for the failure of the French effort was their pursuit of a sea-level rather than a lock canal. Only when he proposed an intricate system of locks, he was opposed by a majority of the congressional members of the Committee on Interoceanic Canals. They still supported the French plan.

With his customary intensity, Roosevelt had followed the debate and studied the two proposals. And once he made up his mind, he set out to get his way. On February 19, 1906, he recommended the lock-canal system to Congress. That June, the Senate formally approved the president's recommendation. The construction of the Panama Canal could now proceed without restraints.

IT WAS A MASSIVE project, but America rolled up its sleeves, opened its Treasury, and threw itself into the task. Roosevelt had been the canal's greatest champion. He had nearly single-handedly pushed a reluctant Congress into action, sent troops to the isthmus, and covertly fermented a revolution. Now that 34,000 workers were toiling in the Panamanian heat to help fulfill his hard-won dream, he decided he must visit. He needed to see with his own eyes what all his years of efforts, his unwavering determination, had brought forth.

In November 1906, Roosevelt became the first sitting president to travel outside the continental United States. He arrived in Panama and he spoke with a heartfelt passion to several hundred American workers and engineers. In his mind, he was the commander in chief addressing front-line troops:

"As I have looked at you and seen you work, seen what you have done and are doing, I have felt just exactly as I would feel to see the big men of our country carrying on a great war."

This "great war," as Roosevelt earnestly called it, would continue for nearly another eight years. More than 25,000 people would die during construction, the majority victims of yellow fever and malaria. The final cost, including French and U.S. investments, was $639 million; the American contribution would be more than half this total sum, approximately $350 million. In August 1914, six months ahead of schedule, the first ship traveled through the locks of the Panama Canal and made its way from the Atlantic to the Pacific Ocean.

THE PANAMA CANAL CHANGED America. It made the United States a stronger, richer, and more militarily secure country. Nearly a century after its completion, the canal continues to return tangible dividends to the nation on a president's daring investment: Each year, over 14,000 ships pass through carrying more than 203 million tons of cargo. A full 10 percent of the nation's entire commercial shipping travels through the canal. Each year America's coastlines are protected and defended by warships that use the canal.

Yet, while the Panama Canal remains a visionary and fruitful public investment brought to fruition largely by the iron will of one man, it is also instructive in a new era of foreign adventures to acknowledge the damage Roosevelt's brazen "big stick" tactics inflicted on America's place in the community of nations. The canal became a tangible symbol of American hegemony, a rallying cry in Latin America for protests against Yankee imperialism.

On December 31, 1999, the United States, hoping to assuage the decades of hostility its self-interested and unlawful conduct in the isthmus had nurtured, ceded control of the canal to Panama.

SEVEN

The Rural Electrification
Administration

FRANKLIN DELANO ROOSEVELT WAS astonished. But as he continued to study the letter in his hand, his surprise and bewilderment quickly turned to anger. It not only made no sense, he decided. It was unfair. Even more infuriating, it was undemocratic.

The year was 1924, and FDR's recent life had been tumultuous—years filled with public defeat and personal disaster. He had resigned as assistant secretary of the Navy to run for vice president, only to lose the election. Then he suffered a mysterious illness that left him paralyzed from the waist down. Despairing, Roosevelt had fled from his sprawling estate in Hyde Park, New

York, to a modest cottage in rural Warm Springs, Georgia, where he hoped the waters might offer a cure for his condition.

He held in his hand the electric bill for his tiny rural Georgia home—and it was four times the bill for his upstate New York mansion. He felt this was deeply wrong.

The cost was not the primary issue. He was a rich man, the heir to both his parents' family fortunes. But despite (or perhaps because of) his wealth, he was a democrat—a believer in the fundamental human right of all Americans regardless of accidents of birth or geography to have the opportunity to fulfill their personal ambitions. He also staunchly believed in America's unique world mission—and that the country's best path to international political and commercial power was to build a nation that offered the advantages of the new century's technology to all its citizens.

The disproportionate electric bill, Roosevelt felt, was tangible firsthand evidence that the major electrical companies were discriminating against farmers and other rural customers. The utilities were complacently ignoring the needs of the nation's country folks, condemning people who lived far from the cities to grinding, arduous lives without the commonplace benefits that electricity brought to most twentieth-century homes and businesses.

As FDR studied his electric bill, thoughts began to take shape in his mind that in time would be pursued with a crusader's zeal. A single galling bill triggered, he later said, "my long study of public utility for electric current and the whole subject of getting electricity into farm homes."

It was a study that after Roosevelt became the thirty-second president would culminate in his leading a shrewdly focused political campaign in Congress to electrify the entire country. The story of Roosevelt's determined fight to bring the benefits of electrical power to previously ignored towns and countryside homes is further evidence of how an inspired and concerned leader can use his personal power and the public's trust to make a momentous investment in America's infrastructure. The results improved individual lives while also significantly increasing the wealth, prestige, and economic competitiveness of the nation.

IN A REMARKABLY SHORT time, electricity had helped to transform much of America. It was, after all, only forty years before the future president's receipt of his unsettling bill that Thomas A. Edison had opened his Pearl Street generating station in lower Manhattan. With the flick of that first switch, electrical current surged to a fortunate fifty-nine customers.

By the 1930s, electricity was on its way to becoming an accepted and commonplace aspect of American urban life: nearly 90 percent of city homes had electricity. And as the electrical grid expanded, as readily accessible power charged through cities and villages, the myriad benefits and consequences of electricity, small and large, created a different nation. A rhythm of daily urban life that once was unimaginable quickly became taken for granted. Machines and appliances hummed, streetlamps and house lights glowed, subways thundered, pumps flushed running water, news and entertainment were broadcast over radios, movies flickered on screens—life in the republic's cities roared with confidence and innovation into the twentieth century. Meanwhile American industry and business, fueled by this new and pervasive technology, grew at a rate that was unmatched in the world.

During these decades, the utility companies that serviced the swiftly expanding urban grids became powerful commercial enterprises. Substantial capital was invested in network construction and massive power generation facilities sprung up. From 1901 to 1932, the electrical utility industry increased by a vigorous 12 percent per year.

In this period of rapid growth, the smaller companies, overwhelmed by the staggering cost of extending service to new customers, often were forced to merge with the larger utilities that had first erected the high-voltage transmission lines. The result was monopolistic: By the late 1920s, three quarters of all the power generated nationwide was controlled by the sixteen largest electric power-holding companies.

These big, investor-owned companies were routinely guided by one principle—the maximization of profit. It made no economic sense, the big companies insisted, to finance the construction of electrical grids in the countryside. The average rural area, after all, offered only five or even fewer power customers per mile. It would be expensive to string power lines to isolated farmsteads. A large capital investment was required, only there was no prospect of any substantial return. The controlling companies, therefore, simply decided not to bring electricity to America's rural areas.

This narrow-minded business determination by a handful of powerful electric companies had significant consequences for the nation. By the thirties, only about 10 percent of all farms had been electrified. While the cities were bustling with the benefits of the new century's technological innovations, rural areas were—literally—left in the dark.

It was a decision—grimly practical and ruthlessly complacent—that created a separate America. This was an America isolated from the surging industrial economy, deprived of household amenities, and ignorant of the new mass culture. Without electricity, daily life was a drudgery. On the average, a farmer spent ten hours a week just carrying water. Plowing, planting, and harvesting crops were largely done with human and animal power. Preserving and cooking food, lighting and heating the home—all were part of the demanding, time-consuming tedium of the rural farm family's day.

But it was not just a hard life in this unelectrified America, it was also an unhealthy one. Poor sanitation and the inability to store food resulted in bad diets and high levels of illness. In the hot, humid southern states, for example, diseases festered in the primitive privies; nearly half the students in southern schools were diagnosed with hookworm.

At a meeting in the late nineteenth century of the Vermont Grange, the state chapter of the nationwide fraternal organization for farmers, an exasperated speaker rose to complain about his plight and that of his fellow rural farmers: "Go into the country and you will find numberless cases of men with poor health, crushed energies, ruined constitutions and stunted souls, and women the slaves of habit of excess of labor."

There were, in the 1930s, 5 million farms without electricity in this other, separate America.

YET, WHILE LIFE IN the countryside was too often a hardscrabble misery, there were many citizens who still wanted an America shaped in part by agrarian values. Rural life, they felt with a Jeffer-sonian passion, was a fundamental strand in the national charac-ter, a source of moral and democratic principles that helped to mold a stronger, fairer, harder working America. If the new gener-ation coming of age in the country were to abandon their parents' farms and flock to the cities, this exodus would have deep and dis-turbing consequences for the nation.

As early as 1908, President Theodore Roosevelt—FDR's fifth cousin—created the Country Life Commission to study rural life and to help make it "as effective and satisfying" as living in the big cities. "I warn my countrymen," he wrote in an article that served as an introduction to the commission's report, "that the great re-cent progress made in city life is not a full measure of our civiliza-tion; for our civilization rests at bottom on the wholesomeness, the attractiveness, and the completeness, as well as the prosperity of life in the country."

The report became a rallying cry for those who wanted rural life to remain part of the American experience, and at the same time it offered a practical agenda for moving farms into the mod-ern era. To raise the farmers' standards of living, it recommended federal hydroelectric projects, rural cooperatives, and "associative efforts" to bring telephone and electric service to the countryside.

To bolster this burgeoning "country life movement," Teddy Roosevelt also created in 1905 the Bureau of Forestry (now the U.S. Forest Service). Its primary purpose was to conserve for fu-ture generations the natural integrity of rural life by preserving forests. Roosevelt appointed Gifford Pinchot, a patrician Yale graduate whose family had made a fortune in lumber, to head the bureau. Only now Pinchot, a great champion of rural life and values, was determined to preserve the natural resources that had created his ancestors' wealth. Working closely with President Roosevelt, he more than tripled the size of the national forests, to a total of 172 million acres in 150 publicly owned tracts.

Celebrated for his success in conserving forests and promoting rural life, Pinchot in 1923 was elected governor of Pennsylvania. As governor, Pinchot remained true to the causes that had helped him get elected. One of his first official acts was to order a "feasibility study for electrifying rural areas of the state."

The survey was called "Giant Power." And its chairman was an inspired appointment: Morris Cooke.

AN ENGINEERING GRADUATE OF Lehigh University, Cooke had previously been director of the Department of Public Works of Philadelphia. It had been a combative directorship as he frequently contested what he believed were the unfair practices of the Philadelphia Electric Company. Now the chairman of the Giant Power study group, he set out in his typically knowledgeable and self-confident way to demonstrate that electric power for the countryside was an affordable and wise investment.

The 1925 Giant Power Report was as visionary as it was uncompromising. It proposed generating power near Pennsylvania's coal mines and a vast statewide network of public-owned and -financed transmission lines that would reach into the state's rural countryside.

The electricity industry moved quickly to counter this bold proposal. Led by its chief spokesman, Herbert Hoover, the secretary of commerce, it issued its own opposition report. Entitled

"SuperPower," this was a manifesto designed to keep the federal government out of the power business and to leave the regulation of utility rates to the state legislatures. Significantly, "SuperPower" simply avoided the entire issue of extending power to rural consumers.

The Pennsylvania legislature considered the two reports—and decided to vote down the Giant Power proposal. It was a decision that in effect decreed that the state's isolated areas would not have electrical service.

There was, however, one salutary consequence of the Giant Power Report. It attracted the attention of the new governor of New York.

OVERCOMING THE DIFFICULTIES RESULTING from his continuing paralysis, Franklin Roosevelt had been elected New York State's governor in 1928. And during his four years in office, inspired in part by his goading experience in Georgia, his study of public utility law at Columbia, and his instinctively democratic political instincts, he constantly challenged the practices of the electrical utilities and their holding companies. To help him in this battle, he appointed Cooke to lead a taskforce that would promote the building of a public hydroelectric plant using the waters of the St. Lawrence River.

Glad to be liberated from his futile efforts in Pennsylvania, Cooke threw himself into his new task. But he never abandoned his commitment to bringing electrical power to the isolated areas of the nation. And as part of his study of the hydroelectrical potential of the St. Lawrence, Cooke also issued a carefully calculated analysis of the cost of erecting powers lines in the countryside.

The electric industry for years had huffed that the price would be prohibitive—at least a daunting $2,000 for every mile. Cooke, however, determined that the actual expense would be much less. Depending on the location and the terrain, the cost of extending the electrical grid would vary between an affordable $300 per mile to at most $1,500, a sum that was still considerably cheaper than the industry estimate.

Cooke's study was released in 1933, and it caused a stir. Rural electrification was now seen by its advocates as not only in the national interest but also affordable.

And when Franklin Delano Roosevelt took office as president in 1933, the supporters of rural electrification finally had the important ally they needed. Life on America's farms, they believed, would soon change dramatically.

THE NEW PRESIDENT WAS a crusader. He brought the New Deal to Washington: a broad program of populist national reforms that were fundamentally, as the historian Albert Fried has perceptively judged, "Roosevelt's attempt to save the members of his own class from the consequences of their folly and avarice." At a cabinet meeting, according to the diaries of Harold Ickes, the interior secretary, a livid Roosevelt had echoed the widely held belief that a cabal-like group of eighty men controlled the nation's business and finances. The president announced that he was "tired of eighty men controlling the destinies of one hundred and twenty million people. . . . The only way to curb their control," he thundered, was "to do away with the holding companies."

It was in this charged atmosphere, a time made hopeful for many Americans by the genuine possibilities of deep, democratic change, that Morris Cooke came to Washington. He went to work as a vaguely titled consultant in the Public Works Administration (PWA). However, his unofficial job was more influential: He advised the president on conservation and power issues. And with Ickes's approval, an optimistic Cooke quickly drew up a plan for a national rural electrification program.

Yet to Cooke's dismay, the president and the cabinet responded to his far-seeing plan with mute disinterest. There were apparently too many large and controversial projects in the works. Besides, the utility companies already were up in arms over the Tennessee Valley Authority (TVA), a large, public power development program on the Tennessee River. While Roosevelt was sympathetic to Cooke's proposal to bring electricity to the countryside, the president simply did not see how in the midst of so many battles he could start another acrimonious political war.

Yet as events unfolded, it would be the TVA's success that ultimately gave both Cooke and Roosevelt the support and confidence they needed to launch their bold national plan.

THE PEOPLE IN THE little town of Alcorn, Mississippi, wanted to enjoy the benefits of twentieth-century life. They wanted lights in their homes, running water in their barns, radios in their front rooms. They wanted electricity, and they wanted it at an affordable rate. The big utility companies could find no practical reason to bring power to Alcorn, but the TVA decided that it would.

The TVA sold power to a regional electric company; then a cooperative formed by the Alcorn townspeople purchased the power at wholesale rates. Service was extended to isolated farms without the usual connection surcharge. As a result of the cooperative's bulk buying, the people in Alcorn were able to bring power into their homes at half the normal price the big, private companies would have charged.

It was a good business deal for all involved. Rural people rushed to sign up for the service. Sales of electrical products boomed in Corinth, the county seat. After only six months, the Alcorn Cooperative's revenues were more than double its expenses—including taxes, interest, depreciation, and overhead. To the astonishment of the big utility companies, which had maintained that extending their grids to the countryside would be a disastrous business practice, the co-op's entire start-up debt to the TVA would be paid off within six years.

By the end of 1934, politicians in Washington were looking at Alcorn. And they were beginning to think that what worked in a little Mississippi town could be successful in other rural areas, too.

SHREWDLY, COOKE MOVED TO take advantage of the well-publicized success in Alcorn. He had been appointed by the president to chair the Mississippi Valley Commission. His mandate was broad: the commission was charged with finding ways to improve life in the valley. But the report that Cooke issued in October 1934 was quite single-minded: it was an impassioned call for rural electrification.

Electricity, Cooke's report categorically declared, was essential for the renewal of country life. It would advance agriculture, generate wealth, and improve the quality of daily life. Using the example of Alcorn, the report called for the federal government to invest $100 million to finance and oversee a national network of rural electrical cooperatives.

As Cooke's dramatic report circulated through the corridors of power in Washington, lobbyists from the American Farm Bureau and the National Grange, the fraternal organization of farmers, quickly went to work to reinforce its message. At a meeting with FDR in the White House, Farm Bureau head Edward O'Neal offered the president blunt advice: "Appoint that big boy from Philadelphia [Cooke] to advise you about rural electrification. That will revolutionize the standard of living of rural people like nothing else could."

And now Roosevelt, encouraged by his perception of a change in public sentiment and the economic success in Alcorn, decided the moment was finally right to act on his long-held desire to help rural Americans. On May 11, 1935, FDR signed an executive order creating the Rural Electrification Administration (REA). It was a $100 million plan predicated on cooperation with the private utilities that would, as part of the government's vast work relief program, bring electrical power to isolated areas of the country.

Morris Cooke was named chief of the REA, with the power to initiate and supervise all its projects. Full of optimism, he exulted that the REA would bring "a complete change to the way of life of the American farm. It will rekindle the interest of our people in farming."

From the start, Cooke realized that if the REA were to succeed he would need the cooperation of the big electric companies. It would not take much persuasion to convince the utilities to extend their power lines to rural communities, he believed. He was convinced they would be his allies in a patriotic plan to reinvent rural American life.

COOKE WAS, AT BEST, naive. For many deeply held reasons, the utilities were categorically opposed to cooperating with the REA.

Cooke did not, for example, accurately gauge the animosity created by the administration's support for what was ominously dubbed the "Death Sentence Bill." Unlike previous attempts at reform, this legislation was not simply an attempt to regulate electrical holding companies. It was a bill designed to tax them out of existence.

The utility industry, of course, fought back. It was determined to undermine what it saw as a radical plan to replace the big companies—and their big profits—with a nationwide group of "little TVAs." Led by its well-funded front organization, the Edison Electric Institute, the industry began a massive lobbying campaign in Congress and at the same time launched a series of lawsuits to defeat the bill and halt rural electrification.

The companies also objected that FDR's executive order had made the REA a work relief agency. A reasonable man, Cooke found himself agreeing with them. It would be too impractical if the REA had to provide help to the unemployed; levels of prior expertise and training were required if the grids were to be successfully extended. So, he met with the president, Ickes, and Secretary of Agriculture Henry Wallace, and shared his concerns. They listened, and agreed: Work relief should not be the REA's central mission. FDR promptly issued a new executive order: The REA would function only as a lending agency.

This compromise did little to assuage the industry's intransigence. Cooke, however, was still sanguine. Convinced that he could demonstrate to the companies the economic viability of bringing power to isolated areas, Cooke publicly challenged them to open "100 test areas."

The companies' response was—silence. They simply ignored Cooke's suggestion. They did not believe that the investment required to wire vast rural stretches of the United States could ever be in their long-term financial interest.

But as Cooke began to lose hope, FDR, tenacious and resourceful, intervened. Determined to break the holding companies' hardheaded and self-interested control of the electrical industry, the president decided it was time to bring some new political muscle to the fight.

IN THE SENATE, GEORGE Norris of Nebraska was the chairman of the Judiciary Committee. Working with FDR, he had helped to shepherd many of the New Deal programs through the chamber. In the House, Sam Rayburn of Texas had employed a mix of folksy populism and personality to persuade normally conservative congressmen to support progressive legislation. Rather than surrender to the holding companies, a resolute FDR in early 1936 recruited these two legislative giants to recast the REA with new funding and a new purpose.

Norris quickly went to work. He introduced an uncompromising bill that would create a permanent REA authorized to spend $1 billion to bring power to rural homes.

The scale of the proposed funding was daunting. A billion dollars was a breathtaking sum in an era when more than a third of all American families had annual incomes under $1,000. In 1936, the average annual per capita spending on utilities was a modest $23, but Norris was suggesting that this sum be increased exponentially—and that public funds be used to make this expenditure possible.

Norris believed with conviction that the federal government should be willing to pay whatever cost would be required to accomplish the essential task of bringing electrical power to the farms. "The farmer," he said, in an attempt to explain the program's colossal price tag, "needs all the facilities which the city dweller needs, but in addition thereto he needs many facilities for which the city dweller has no use . . . electric current to grind feed, to pump water and to perform other services."

Norris also enlisted Cooke to help explain to a skeptical Senate why the nation could not depend on the electric companies, but instead must turn to a federal program. In a letter to the Agriculture Committee supporting the Senate bill, an angry Cooke shared the conclusion he had reached after his own frustrating experiences in Pennsylvania and with the REA: "The policy of the utility companies has been to skim the cream of the business. Such a policy has precluded the extension of service to nearly 90 percent of American farms and been paralyzing in its effect."

Still, many senators continued to object to the tremendous cost of this new REA. Roosevelt, who when the situation required could be as practical as he was often idealistic, decided it was necessary to reduce the proposed funding. He agreed to a compromise plan that would make $420 million—still a colossal expenditure in 1936—available to the REA over ten years.

With that revision, on February 15, 1936, the Senate Agriculture Committee approved the Norris bill for rural electrification.

A MONTH LATER, THE House Committee on Interstate and Foreign Commerce chaired by Sam Rayburn held hearings on the REA bill. Cooke was the chief witness.

Cooke's performance was masterful. Fortified by his years of hands-on experience and his deep knowledge of the industry and its technologies, Cooke for three long days patiently parried the congressmen's probing questions.

He also worked effectively to assuage some of the conservative legislators' deeper fears of how the precedent of a federally financed REA program might reshape American democracy. Connecticut congressman Schuyler Merritt, the only Republican elected to Congress in the 1932 Roosevelt landslide who had run against an incumbent Democrat, offered up a sarcastic—and contemptuous—challenge. He wanted to know if Cooke was looking forward "to having the federal government extend its hand into every county in the United States?"

"In helping finance them, you mean," Cooke replied evenly.

"Yes," said Merritt. "And once they get in, they will want to run the whole nation."

Relentlessly, Merritt continued to try to trap Cooke into asserting that the REA was the precursor of more extensive federal control. Did Cooke, the congressman asked in his final question, think it would be a good thing if "the federal government takes over the electric business all over the United States?"

"It would be a calamity," Cooke, a model of calm and reasonableness, replied. With that judicious response, much of the conservative opposition was deflated.

There were, however, other representatives who were determined to impugn Cooke's testimony. One jingoistic committee member became enraged by Cooke's matter-of-fact revelation that the United States was behind other countries in electrification. With a building anger, he repeatedly questioned the accuracy of this statistic. At last, Chairman Rayburn intervened.

"Let us take my county, where I live," suggested Rayburn in his seemingly casual, backcountry Texas way. "There are 5,894 farms in that county," he announced with a disarming precision. "Farms in the neighborhood of 90 acres . . . a house practically every mile, maybe more. Out of those 5,894 farms, there are 94 that are electrified."

That quieted the doubting congressman. And with Norris and Rayburn's strong and effective leadership, once the REA bill managed to make its way through the initial contentious committee vetting, it proceeded to move swiftly through both chambers. In both the House and the Senate, there was surprisingly little debate. The Norris-Rayburn bill passed with broad support in May 1936.

The new REA would implement a ten-year plan to provide twenty-five-year loans at 3 percent to public entities—farmers' or-

ganizations, municipalities, and public power and utility districts—
that would bring electric power to rural areas. It would be one of
the largest capital investment projects of the New Deal.

After the years spent battling the highly organized utility
companies, after being frustrated by the ineffectiveness of his initial executive order, on May 21, 1936, Franklin Roosevelt signed
the Rural Electrification Act into law. It had taken the president
twelve combative years, but at last he had been able to respond
effectively to the galling electric bill he had received for his rural
Georgia cottage.

ON A WARM JULY day in 1936, Morris Cooke stood on the porch of
a Virginia farm not far from Washington, D.C. Its fields had been
under cultivation since the time of George Washington, and
"Stonewall" Jackson and Robert E. Lee had once dined at the farm-
house table. Now this country homestead—and rural America,
too—was about to enter a new era.

As two hundred assembled guests watched, Harold Ickes
threw a switch. In that instant, electrical current flowed into the
old house. A refrigerator, a dishwasher, air conditioners, an electric range—all the marvels of modern domestic life suddenly were
operational. In the barns, electric brooders for hens, feed grind-
ers, and milk coolers surged with power.

Cooke watched proudly as one farm and one family were happily brought into the comfort of the twentieth century. But he also
understood this was only the start. Rural homesteads throughout
the entire nation would soon enjoy the comforts and innovations
that electricity brought to everyday life.

Within the first two years of the REA's operation, 1.5 million farms in 45 states received electrical power from 350 cooperatives. Over the subsequent decades, the electrical grid continued to expand. By the 1950s, the REA had provided power to nearly all American farms. The default rate on REA loans during all those years was negligible—under 1 percent.

As electricity came to isolated parts of the country, families and communities were brought into the mainstream of American cultural and economic life. The intense privation and grueling drudgery of farm life disappeared. Thousands of new jobs took root in a countryside where appliances and plumbing were soon commonplace. And as radios and later televisions and phonographs appeared in even the most isolated of homes, the educational and cultural divides between urban and rural America began to shrink. An electrified America was a stronger, better-educated, more prosperous, and more democratic republic.

The campaign had stretched on for nearly three decades, and throughout, Franklin Delano Roosevelt had tenaciously led the way. He was a leader with a deeply democratic vision, an idealist willing to write new laws and invest government funds to maximize the potential for a better and fairer life for all Americans. At the same time, he was a pragmatic politician, a man who knew the necessity of strategic compromises and the value of delegating authority to well-chosen associates. He was a president determined to lead the nation into a more egalitarian future. With the Rural Electrification Administration—a public investment that was innovative, transforming, and fiercely fair—he demonstrated how a determined leader can leave an enduring legacy to the nation.

EIGHT

The Reconstruction Finance Corporation

FEW WORDS WERE SPOKEN as the two grim men sat in the back of the limousine driving down Pennsylvania Avenue. It was Inauguration Day, March 4, 1933, and President-elect Franklin Delano Roosevelt shared the rear seat with an openly hostile Herbert Hoover, the incumbent president he had defeated and would shortly be replacing. Earlier that morning, the desperate governors of Illinois and New York had ordered the closing of banks in Chicago and New York City; in the panic that followed, other financial institutions had quickly barred their doors, too. By the time the limousine carrying its two bristling passengers reached the Capitol for the ceremony where Roosevelt would be sworn in as the nation's thirty-second president, America's banking system had shut down.

Each man blamed the other for the severity of the crisis. A day earlier, Roosevelt had made the traditional visit by the president-elect to the Oval Office only to find to his surprise that Hoover was waiting with his Treasury secretary and the head of the Federal Reserve. Hoover and his economic team implored Roosevelt to unite with them in an immediate bipartisan response to the nation's looming financial catastrophe. It was an appeal that was reminiscent of the letter Hoover had sent a month earlier to Roosevelt asking the president-elect to join the White House in assuring the public that the banking crisis would be resolved. Roosevelt had dismissed the president's letter as a "cheeky document," scoffing at the wishful prospect of rhetoric's having any impact on such an entrenched economic disaster. On the day before his inauguration, Roosevelt had once again adamantly refused to take any action in conjunction with Hoover.

Yet, while America's banking crisis had escalated perilously during this tense, uncooperative presidential interregnum, the Roosevelt administration would nevertheless demonstrate how a forceful leader can innovatively build on his predecessor's accomplishments. It was Herbert Hoover who had established the Reconstruction Finance Corporation (RFC) in the midst of the depression to lend federal capital to failing private businesses. And it was Franklin Delano Roosevelt who, despite his own disdain for Hoover, had the bold vision to expand the RFC and transform the agency into the crucial financial engine that would drive the New Deal, and in the process help revitalize an economically battered

America. What these two very different presidents accomplished with the RFC is, in its unique bipartisan way, another example of how determined activist leaders can use federal funds to make massive investments to rebuild the country—and further evidence that the longtime payoff from these shrewd (and often unprecedented) investments can be the creation of a more prosperous, stronger, and more self-sustaining America.

HERBERT HOOVER TOOK AN unlikely path to the presidency. The son of a Quaker blacksmith, Hoover was born in an Iowa village and was orphaned by the age of nine. Yet he was smart and ambitious, and succeeded in making his way through Stanford University. He earned a geology degree, went to work as a mining engineer in Australia and China, and in time used his expertise and drive to earn his own fortune.

Wealthy, a globalist by experience, and an instinctive philanthropist, Hoover was recruited by President Woodrow Wilson to head the American Food Administration. During World War I, he galvanized the nation to reduce its consumption of foodstuffs in order to help provide rations for soldiers. After the war, he organized shipments of food for the starving millions in Central Europe, and, in spite of bitter opposition from Henry Cabot Lodge and other Senate Republicans, also arranged vital food deliveries to defeated Germany and Bolshevist Russia.

The well-publicized successes of these food and aid programs led to Hoover's being appointed first by President Warren Harding and then by President Calvin Coolidge as secretary of commerce. An entrepreneur who had made his fortune as a wild-catting engineer, he was supportive of the laissez-faire "New Era" economic policies of the late 1920s championed by both presidents. It was a confident time when many believed, as Harding had pugnaciously asserted, that "what this country needs is less government in business and more business in government." Similarly, Hoover thought that the nation could be viewed as a "single, industrial organism," and that federal intervention in business practices should simply be as "a promoter and educator."

When in 1927 Coolidge decided not to run for a second full term, Hoover's accomplishments and popularity earned him the Republican presidential nomination on the first ballot. He campaigned as a friend of big business and took credit for the apparently booming economy. "We in America are nearer to the final triumph over poverty than ever before in the history of any land," he pledged as he went around the country. In November 1928, Hoover was elected the thirty-first president of the United States.

But by the time Hoover took office in March 1929, the nation was in big trouble. The stock market would soon crash. Farms had been losing internal markets as European agriculture revived, and then in the summer of 1930 a severe drought devastated the crops planted in the heartland. As the farm economy struggled, rural credit concerns weakened and finally broke: from 1921 to 1929, at least 5,000 small-town banks suspended operations. This disaster impacted on the larger, urban banks: In 1930, an additional 1,350 banks throughout the country failed. Railroads, already feeling competitive pressure from airlines and motor vehicles, now lost further revenues as the unsteady economy caused fewer people to travel and less freight to be shipped. As a result, by 1933, more than 750,000 railroad employees would be laid off, while railroad securities, previously a seemingly safe investment, plummeted. Within a year, unemployment jumped from 5 million in 1930 to a staggering 11 million. The nation was in a deep, downwardly spiraling economic depression.

Treasury Secretary Andrew Mellon, an advocate of the era's laissez-faire approach to business, lectured that the government's response to this economic free fall should be to "leave it alone." Hoover, too, believed in the fundamental strength of the nation's economy and its ability to correct itself. He remained reluctant to pursue federal legislative relief. Instead, he advocated voluntary restrictions and encouraged state and local governments to deal with the financial problems confronting their citizens.

But as the Great Depression deepened and as daily life turned into a nasty struggle for more and more Americans, Hoover realized that the federal government would need to intervene. Even the financial community, reeling and demoralized, was ready to abandon its laissez-faire approach to capitalism. Bankers urged the administration to reestablish the War Finance Corporation, which had been created by Congress in 1918 to offer financial support to wartime industries and to the banks that helped capitalize them. Driven to a resigned pragmatism by the country's desperate mood, Hoover decided that he could support Congress's taking short-term actions to build confidence—as long as these steps would not "inflict upon the country a collectivist economy" or "destroy personal liberty."

ON DECEMBER 7, 1931, President Herbert Hoover asked Congress to address the economic crisis facing the nation by creating "an emergency reconstruction program." Based on the War Finance Corporation, this new agency would primarily provide credit to liquefy the assets of failing banks. The corporation would not be used, the president reassuringly explained, "very extensively." It would strengthen confidence in the economy and, he predicted with a convincing certainty, it would be liquidated within a brief two years.

Yet despite Hoover's carefully restrained tone, many Americans were astonished by the prospect of the Reconstruction Finance Corporation. The president was asking that $2 billion in federal funds be provided for loans to private businesses. In the midst of the Great Depression, this was an enormous amount of money; in fact, under his predecessor Calvin Coolidge, the entire federal budget had been less than $3 billion.

As conservative commentators warned that this emergency reconstruction program would be "the beginning of state socialism," liberal and progressive Democrats attacked with a fury inspired by different concerns. Congressman Fiorello LaGuardia of New York called the legislation "a millionaire's dole . . . a subsidy for broken bankers [and] bankrupt railroads . . . a reward for speculation and unscrupulous bond pluggers." Pennsylvania representative Louis McFadden charged that the RFC Act was "a scheme for taking . . . the people's money . . . and giving it to a supercorporation for the sinister purpose of helping a gang of financial looters cover their tracks." And in the Senate, Robert Wagner of New York, who under pressure from his state's bankers would ultimately vote for the bill, complained that the act offered little that was tangible for the millions of unemployed Americans.

But Hoover was determined to rally support for the bill—within limits. His handling of the economic crisis has been characterized by David Burner, an astute biographer, as "a curious mixture of boldness and hesitation," and his public endorsements of the RFC Act were typically vacillating. On the one hand, Hoover promised that the bill would create "a powerful organization . . . to strengthen weaknesses" in "our credit, banking and railroad structure," while with the other restraining hand, he stressed that the RFC was "not created for the aid of big industries or big banks" which could "take care of themselves."

The new political reality though, was, that the RFC Act was unprecedented. With $500 million of capital and authorization to borrow an additional $1.5 billion from the Treasury, it made substantial government assistance available to the entire U.S. financial marketplace. It could operate for as long as ten years, although its lending authorization would need to be renewed by Congress in two years. And, as enumerated in James Stuart Olson's seminal study, the corporation could make loans to a myriad of entities suffering from the Great Depression's sting: "commercial banks, saving banks, insurance companies, trust companies, building and loan associations, mortgage loan companies, credit unions, Federal Land banks, joint stock land banks, Federal Intermediate Credit banks, agricultural credit corporations, livestock credit corporations, receivers of closed banks, and railroads."

Anxious opponents of the bill charged that the RFC would recast the federal government's relationship with the private sector. But the vast majority of the legislators knew their constituents were eager for a dramatic intervention to rescue the besieged

American economy. The RFC Act sailed triumphantly through Congress: the House vote was an overwhelming 355 to 5, and the Senate tally a no less impressive 63 to 8.

Only a little more than a month after he had proposed the bill, on January 22, 1932, President Herbert Hoover signed the Reconstruction Finance Act into law.

AN ERA OF ENORMOUS federal involvement in private business began. Funds from the U.S. Treasury now began to flow into the ailing economy. The RFC's strategy was to concentrate on shoring up the larger financial entities; the theory was that their collapse would reverberate disastrously throughout the marketplace. Therefore, out of the nation's more than 24,000 banks, only the large institutions received loans. The RFC also focused on saving the large railroads whose bonds were primarily held by insurance companies and banks. By curtailing bank suspensions and preventing the collapse of the railroad bond market, Hoover hoped the RFC would steady the listing credit market.

In its first two months, the RFC loaned an impressive quarter-billion dollars. Bank failures eased off in February and March 1932. But business owners and consumers were still wary; and as investments and spending remained stalled, the perception continued that the nation remained inextricably mired in the Great Depression. By May, frustrated Democrats in Congress began to attack the RFC for its failure to revive the economy.

Then, in June, the Central Republic Bank of Chicago teetered on the brink of collapse. Urged on by Jesse Jones, the brash Texas Democratic political operator and RFC board member, the agency rushed to the bank's rescue with a $90 million loan. It was another substantial loan to a major institution; more than one third of the entire $950 million the corporation loaned to banks and trust companies in 1932 went to only twenty-six institutions. And now the public began to complain. Editorials charged that the RFC's loan policies were unfair and undemocratic. When it was widely reported that a Chicago municipal employee lost his home after he could not pay a $34 tax because the financially strapped city was unable to give him $850 in back pay, the apparent inequities in the government's relief program were starkly dramatized: big banks and big bankers were saved, while civil servants could not get the money the cities owed them. Hoover, hissed a growing national chorus, was simply a friend of the rich.

By the uneasy summer of 1932, large segments of the American population had grown increasingly apprehensive. RFC loans of more than $1 billion had improved the financial marketplace, but the effects of this massive infusion of federal funds had not trickled down to the unemployed millions. Life for too many remained a desperate struggle. Hunger marches took place in cities throughout the country. And then in June and July, a "Bonus Army" defiantly marched on Washington.

Twenty thousand strong, the Bonus Expeditionary Force (BEF) was made up of World War I veterans and their families who demanded immediate payment of a veterans' bonus that had been approved by Congress in 1924 but was not scheduled to be distributed until 1945. The veterans and their families wanted— and needed—the promised payment now. They flocked to Washington, camping out in thousands of tents erected on the city's central Mall, with the hope of influencing Congress.

It was a tense time in the city; and each day that passed without Congress's taking action hardened the veterans' animosities. When violence between marchers and police broke out and two veterans were killed, Hoover decided he needed to act before the volatile situation escalated completely out of control. Disperse the protestors, he ordered.

Led by Major George S. Patton, U.S. Army troops charged into the ranks of their own veterans. "Shame! Shame!" taunted the crowds. Hoover, too, was shocked. He instructed the Army to withdraw. But the operation's commander, General Douglas Mac-Arthur, ignored the president's new order. Infantry attacked the BEF encampment—and in the assault two infants were killed and there were numerous casualties.

In the mournful aftermath of this attack by American troops on American citizens, Hoover began to appreciate (and perhaps even fear) the nation's unsteady mood. It was an election year, but this was more than a personal political calamity. He decided that the federal government must take action to help the millions of unemployed Americans.

CHARITY AND HUMANITARIAN AID, Hoover had previously tersely insisted, would be sufficient to handle the needs of the country's unfortunate. He was philosophically opposed to direct federal relief for the unemployed. And this hardheaded position was seconded by his RFC chairman, Eugene Meyer. Despite the growing demands from a concerned Congress, the California Republican remained dead-set against expanding the RFC mission to include welfare or public works.

But in this period of national crisis, Hoover finally realized that philosophy was not as crucial as jobs. He moved forward with two decisive acts. First, he replaced the recalcitrant Meyer with Atlee Pomerence, a Democrat from Ohio whose appointment gave that party a majority on the corporation board. Next, the president proposed a revolutionary public works and relief bill to Congress.

The Emergency Relief and Construction Act, like the original RFC bill, was an unprecedented advance in federally funded public policy. It provided $300 million for RFC loans to states and another $1.5 billion to finance "self-liquidating" (i.e., that automatically pay down) public works projects. The bill also included funds for low-cost housing and $36 million for the besieged regional agricultural credit corporations. The U.S. Treasury would be injecting substantial amounts into the economy for new construction and the activist hope was that the projects would create needed jobs. In July 1932, an optimistic Hoover signed the Emergency Relief and Construction Act into law.

Yet despite the program's generously funded intentions, a series of ill-advised specifics in the bill's fine print hampered its effectiveness. For example, at the insistence of John Nance Garner, the Democratic Speaker of the House, the bill stated that the RFC identify the recipients of its loans. This requirement made even the most needy bankers reluctant to borrow: they feared a public announcement would highlight their straits and precipitate the panic they were hoping to avoid.

Another unforeseen problem occurred when RFC chairman Pomerence established a "Self-Liquidating Division" to deal in a systematic manner with the anticipated deluge of requests for public works and relief loans. As expected, a flurry of requests poured in. Only now the new division initiated lengthy reviews and detailed engineering studies for each proposed public works project so that future income could be predicted. As the evaluations dragged on and rigorously on, the vast majority of requests remained proposals rather than actual construction projects. Few new jobs were created.

Similarly, the "Emergency Relief Division" of the RFC was funded with a seemingly lavish $300 million. In just its first day of operation, though, it received requests from five states totaling $200 million. Overwhelmed, the RFC began "rationing" its capital. This was prudent, but it also was a caution that served to reinforce the angry public's perception that the agency willingly lent bankers fantastic sums while millions of unemployed Americans starved.

The agency's new "Agricultural Credit Division" also moved forward with mixed results. It made $37 million in loans and distributed an additional $130 million through the Department of Agriculture that helped, according to a prideful government, "tens of thousands of farmers." Yet the RFC loans to farmers and crop distributors were offered at a dauntingly high 7 percent. If the interest rate had been set at a more realistic, affordable level, the number of applicants would have greatly increased—and more struggling farmers could have received the financial assistance they needed.

Still, even with all its faults, the accomplishments of Hoover's RFC were significant. Through the Railway Credit Corporation, the agency helped shaky railroads with $300 million in loans. It funded the construction of sewage systems, waterworks, and railroad bridges throughout the country, and many of these public works continue to provide benefits to this day. For example, it was the RFC that capitalized the construction of the San Francisco–Oakland Bay Bridge; the Metropolitan Aqueduct that brings water from the Colorado River to Los Angeles; and the development of the public park at Jones Beach, Long Island.

But it was all taking too long. The RFC had by 1932 distributed a colossal $2 billion in loans and had set in motion a plan to arrest the depression's hold on the economy, but an impatient and out-of-work America wanted immediate and tangible results. Hoover still largely believed the depression was a short-term economic bump, and that once the credit market was energized with new capital and bankers' confidence was restored, the nation would be set back on track. He was reluctant to concede that its economic problems were pervasive and that its entire capitalistic system had stalled. He lacked both the perception to see the large, systemic problems and the commander's charisma necessary to mobilize the country to deal with demoralizing and frightening times. When Hoover nevertheless ran for election in November 1932, the beleaguered electorate soundly gave him a vote of no-confidence. He received less than 40 percent of the popular vote, and a mere 59 Electoral College votes. Franklin Delano Roosevelt was swept into office.

"THE GREAT ENGINEER," ELLIOTT Roosevelt, FDR's son, would derisively write about Hoover, "set up the Reconstruction Finance Corporation with . . . pathetic results." But although it is understandable (and forgivable) that a loyal son would give history a sneering twist with the hope of aggrandizing a father's legacy, it is an assessment that is both fatuous and inaccurate. The reality is that Hoover, to his credit, had provided his successor with a unique federal agency already capitalized with huge amounts of money, and able to operate without needing Congress to approve its funding programs. And that FDR, to his credit, realized the unprecedented flexibility in the RFC. In a time of great economic uncertainty, Roosevelt turned the corporation into one of the most powerful agencies in the history of the federal government: the spigot that poured out the enormous sums funding the New Deal.

Roosevelt went to work immediately—not that the banking crisis that had exploded across the nation on the very day of his inauguration had left him much choice. On Sunday, March 5, FDR huddled at the Treasury Department with his own economic advisers and a group of former Hoover administration officials. The next day—the president's first day in the Oval Office—he acted with an exhilarating swiftness. At a specially convened session of Congress, he declared a four-day bank holiday. Then, speaking with an impressive and affecting confidence, he gave a radio address to the nation. He asked Americans to rally together in this economic crisis with the sort of unquestioning patriotic sacrifice and support they would give to the country and its commander in chief in wartime.

The following day, there was further decisive presidential action. Roosevelt sent the Emergency Banking Relief Act to the Hill. Caught up in this whirlwind of activity, Congress passed the act that same day.

Conceived by Hoover's economic team, yet pushed forward

by the power of FDR's personality, the new law was an authoritative federal plan to restore stability to the money markets. It granted the comptroller of the currency power of receivership over national banks that were on the verge of failure and then the right to reorganize them. The new law also authorized the RFC to purchase bank preferred stock, capital notes and debentures, and to use bank stock as loan collateral—all with the hope that these federal dollars would provide banks with investment funds and relieve their short-term government debt. Further, the act institutionalized the national bank holiday and provided that banks would reopen only after federal inspectors declared them secure.

Three days after the passage of this remarkable bill, 5,000 banks received permission to open their doors. Within a short time, two thirds of the country's banks were back in business. Over the next two years, in 1933 and 1934, the RFC would assist 6,800 banks by purchasing preferred stock, notes, and bonds—and in the process pump billions of invigorating dollars back into the moribund economy.

AND THIS WAS JUST the beginning. Unlike the reluctant Hoover, Roosevelt did not envision the RFC as either a temporary relief agency or one whose primary mission should be simply to stabilize the money markets. The entire economy needed to be jumpstarted, and FDR wanted an activist RFC to spread government capital and federally backed credit to as broad a base as possible. To direct this activist Keynesian revival of the economy, the president appointed Jesse Jones, an RFC board member under Hoover, the head of the corporation.

It was an inspired choice. The son of a tobacco farmer, Jones started out working in a uncle's Houston lumberyard, and, driven by diligence, ambition, and intelligence, went on to earn—and happily spend—several fortunes. Jones was in rapid succession a timber and real estate magnate, hotel builder, owner of the *Houston Chronicle*, finance director of the Democratic National Committee, chairman of the Texas Trust Committee, president of the National Bank of Commerce, and a major shareholder in the Humble Oil Company. He was a staunch conservative who railed against wasteful government spending, and many of FDR's progressive policies left him uneasy. But he was also an empire builder and he perceptively saw in the RFC an opportunity to create a well-funded powerhouse that could reach out to rebuild a struggling America.

Assisted by Thomas Corcoran, a jovial, young Harvard-educated attorney in the RFC's General Counsel's Office, Jones turned the agency into a well-staffed and efficient operation. Its talented lawyers, comptrollers, bank examiners, personnel and public relations experts were ready to be deployed around the country to handle any crisis.

When, in 1934, Congress renewed the RFC's authorization and in the process put another $850 million into the agency's coffers, Jones had the funding to realize his ambitions. Still not satisfied, he persuaded Roosevelt to approve the RFC's additional right to spend its incoming loan payments. He disdained the Wall Street conservatism that had mitigated Hoover's view of the RFC. He wanted the agency to reflect the same sort of brash shrewdness that had molded his own financial success. And now with a fortune at his command, Jones set out to invest it in the nation.

• • •

JONES BELIEVED THAT THE RFC should save the entire banking system. To accomplish this lofty goal, Jones was determined to use the RFC to guarantee that banks' assets exceeded their liabilities—regardless of how much money the RFC would need to distribute in the process. He wanted to ensure that as many institutions as possible would be eligible for membership in the newly created Federal Deposit Insurance Corporation (FDIC) when it opened in January 1934. He launched a national public relations campaign to persuade bankers to issue preferred stock, which they would then sell to the RFC to increase their institutions' loanmaking abilities.

His programs were a tremendous success. By September 1934, the RFC, according to its own assessment, owned stock in about half the nation's banks. Within the year, 14,400 banks had joined the FDIC. And bank deposits had ballooned to $44 billion—$7 billion higher than when FDR called for the emergency bank holiday following his inauguration. By 1935, the money markets had finally stabilized.

But banks were not the only beneficiaries of the RFC. FDR and Jones were intent on restoring stability to the entire economy. Like a rich uncle, Jones lavished government funds on the New Deal agencies run by his regular poker-playing Washington buddies. The Federal Emergency Relief Administration Fund (FERA), led by Harry Hopkins, received $1.5 billion in RFC funding to provide relief grants. Harold Ickes's Public Works Administration greatly expanded its construction portfolio thanks to Jones's distributing RFC dollars. Other innovative New Deal agencies that helped to transform the nation were also enthusiastically financed by Jones's broad-ranging RFC: the Rural Electrification Administration received $246 million; the Resettlement Administration got $175 million; and the Federal Home Loan Bank was funded with $125 million.

Farmers, too, were targeted in the widespread federally funded recovery. The Commodity Credit Corporation (CCC), funded with $1.6 billion from the RFC, was created in October 1933. Designed to raise farmers' incomes and the price of their products, the CCC granted loans with crops as collateral. If prices rose, then the loans could of course be repaid. But if they fell, the CCC would store the crops until the market improved. By the time the CCC had become a permanent agency of the Department of Agriculture in 1939, it had made loans to 4 million farmers.

The RFC also helped to finance the Electric Home and Farm Authority (EHFA), an inventive consumer-oriented program established by the president in December 1933 to increase the demand for power in rural areas. If people living in the countryside could purchase gas and electrical appliances at low cost, the manipulative thinking that set up the EHFA reasoned, then they'd certainly want electricity. And this strategy worked. By the time it was disbanded in 1942, the EHFA had financed the sale of more than a million electric appliances to rural homes—and in the process helped to create a new community of consumers for electricity.

Foreign trade, too, was stimulated by the RFC. The agency provided about $200 million in capital and loans to the Export–Import Bank, which, in early 1934, the Roosevelt administration had created to promote trade with the Soviet Union. When a second Export–Import Bank was established to fund trade with other nations and the two banks merged in 1936, the RFC continued its crucial role as a major investor. It purchased $10 million of this new entity's preferred stock.

Disaster relief and recovery was another of the RFC's priorities. It spun off the Disaster Loan Corporation, an agency created to help victims of natural catastrophes. Thirty-five million dollars in low-interest federal loans were distributed to help ravaged communities rebuild after hurricanes, forest fires, tornadoes, and floods.

When legislation to again extend the RFC passed in January 1935, this continuance, thanks to the lobbying of Jones and the president, also granted the agency several impressive new powers. One of the added provisions allowed the corporation to establish a mortgage bank that would capitalize the mortgage market and fund new construction. Another stipulation allowed the agency to buy railroad securities and equipment trust certificates. Acting quickly, Jones invested hundreds of millions of dollars to assist deteriorating railroads to finance their debts and repair or acquire equipment.

Encouraged by FDR and implemented by Jones, the federal government had in just three years funneled a previously unimaginable treasure of funds into the nation's economy. The RFC had become the largest investor in the country, the guarantor of billions of dollars in loans, and the powerful holder of voting rights in thousands of American corporations.

NOT UNEXPECTED, THIS PROGRAM of massive—and revolutionary—government investment had its congressional critics. The most significant challenge to Jones and his free-spending RFC policies, however, came from a member of the president's own cabinet.

Henry Morgenthau, the secretary of the Treasury, was a wealthy and loyal longtime friend and adviser to FDR. But he was also openly skeptical about the cost of the New Deal initiatives. Unlike many of the administration activist economists, Morgenthau was not a Keynesian. He strongly believed in balancing the federal budget, holding down deficits, increasing private economic investments, and, not least, curtailing what he saw as a freewheeling and promiscuously spending RFC. With a fierce inevitability, Morgenthau and Jones became rivals, two confident and powerful men grappling for the trust and support of the one man whose authority and prestige exceeded their own—the president of the United States.

Morgenthau was both a canny and a relentless adversary. He openly drew the battle lines, informing the president that he might be unable to continue to serve as secretary of the Treasury if Roosevelt "did not begin to show some signs of economic sense and interest in curtailing government expenditures." He wanted, he announced, to eliminate the RFC.

At the same contentious time, it was becoming clear that Jones, with his usual soaring certitude, had grossly overestimated the demand for mortgage loans, direct credit, and Export–Import Bank loans. Only $140 million in such loans had been dispersed— far less that the $700 million the RFC, with its unrealistic optimism about the availability of private credit, had publicly anticipated. With a coy vindictiveness, Morgenthau trumpeted this failure to his old friend, the president.

By mid-1935, Roosevelt was beginning to be persuaded. He stepped back a bit from his original crusader's zeal and endorsed Morgenthau's call for deficit reductions and spending cuts. In July, the president decided the RFC should stop buying preferred stock and capital notes. Throughout 1936, as the economy seemed ready to jump back to life, the need for the RFC continued to diminish. The following year, a gloating Morgenthau got the significant budget cuts he had long been championing. And in October 1937, the president agreed that the time for economic prudence had returned. Roosevelt ordered Jones to stop making loans. The RFC, the president declared, was to be closed as quickly as possible.

BUT THE RFC'S DEMISE was short-lived. Without the injection of billions of federal dollars into the marketplace, the country in 1937 and 1938 fell back into a recession. John Maynard Keynes, the British economist, patiently lectured FDR that the reason for the 1936 upswing in the economy was a direct result of the RFC; it had stabilized the money markets and made invigorating investments in public works and employment programs. And this scholarly exposition was reinforced by a more vocal one. In February 1938, operators of a thousand small businesses went to the White House to protest the cutoff of RFC assistance.

Roosevelt, always attentive to the public's mood, was now convinced. He ordered Jones to restart the RFC. An ebullient Jones boasted that "the federal credit establishment might exist indefinitely." In April 1938, the power of agency was once again expanded when the president signed legislation that allowed the

RFC to make loans to self-liquefying construction projects that had an automatic timetable for paying down the borrowed monies incorporated into the loans just as it had done years earlier before the existence of the PWA.

Yet, once again, the RFC's success soon seemed to be leading to its own destruction. The economy rebounded, and by early 1940 appeared once more to be stabilizing. With a well-timed persistence, Morgenthau reiterated his argument that long-term prosperity could only be attained if federal deficits were wiped out—and the elimination of the RFC was the essential first step in this program of fiscal responsibility. "Bookkeeping, nothing more," shot back a dismissive Jones. But the mood in the country was changing. It appeared that the RFC would be shut down again. And this time the closure would be permanent.

Then, in May 1940, Hitler invaded the Low Countries and France.

WORLD WAR II FURTHER centralized the RFC's role in shaping and revitalizing the national economy. With its funding and extralegislative power already in place, the agency became the government's vehicle for much of the public economy and defense spending that fueled the war. It provided the stream of capital for the men and machines that defeated both the Axis powers and, at last, the Great Depression.

In June 1940, Roosevelt signed a bill that authorized the RFC to make loans or purchase stock in any company that produced or transported war materiel. The EHFA and the RFC Mortgage Company were closed, and now the wartime corporation was no longer primarily a recovery agency. The RFC returned to its roots, functioning like a supercharged version of the War Finance Corporation upon which it had been originally modeled. It began to provide capital for billions in defense contracts.

Jesse Jones quickly understood the opportunity—and the patriotic urgency—as the nation went to war, and he used the RFC funds inventively. He created eight RFC subsidiaries for defense production, and their activities were wide-ranging. For example, the Rubber Reserve Company became the nation's only importer of crude rubber. The Rubber Development Corporation helped to produce synthetic rubber, and became the United States primary postwar source for rubber. The Metals Reserve Company spent $2.75 billion to acquire and stockpile strategic metals. While the Defense Plant and Defense Supplies corporations would *each* invest over $9 billion as the nation prepared for war and then fought in Europe and the Pacific.

The wartime RFC was active on other fronts, too. Agency loans financed war damage insurance programs, provided the credit needed to finance new home construction for defense plant workers, and helped build oil pipelines stretching from Texas to New Jersey so that tankers could be available for more strategic duties.

By war's end, the RFC had disbursed a colossal $37 billion. It was an investment that not only helped to win the war but also permanently stabilized the economy. And it was this massive and revolutionary infusion of federal capital into a lumbering marketplace that set the economic stage for America's postwar boom.

• • •

IN THE POSTWAR PERIOD, the RFC began to play a smaller role in the nation's economy. Between 1946 and 1953, the agency continually cut back its dispersal of funds, its annual lending only exceeding $1 billion in 1949. And its subsidiaries began either to wind down their activities or to become separate agencies. The Defense Plant Corporation, for example, sold off its facilities to private industries, including the DuPont Chemical Corporation. The Small Business Administration (SBA) was created to replace the RFC as the lender to local businesses. The Commodity Credit Corporation continued to support farmers, but now as an independent agency. And Fannie Mae became a private corporation; in time, it would become the foremost mortgage lender in the nation.

In 1953, President Dwight D. Eisenhower signed the legislation starting the process that would in four years permanently end the RFC.

CREATED DURING A DEPRESSION, the RFC was the unprecedented economic tool that guided America through rocky economic times, periods of recovery, war, stability, expansion, and prosperity. It was the essential instrument that two very different presidents used not only to rescue America but also to transform and rebuild the country.

"It is important for government and its representatives to realize the essential nature of business enterprise in this country," Jesse Jones had advised the nation in 1939. "As it is for businessmen to get it through their heads that government is in business to stay."

It was a prescriptive wisdom; and this insight, molded out of the activist economic lessons Jones and the nation had learned from the success of the RFC, is no less relevant today as America moves into the twenty-first century.

NINE

The G.I. Bill

W HO THE HELL IS Warren Atherton . . . ?"
That was the angry question posed in a letter to *Time*
magazine in December 1943.

The correspondent was responding to *Time*'s report of the
most recent threat Atherton had made in his very public campaign to obtain benefits for World War II veterans: "We'll start a
bonfire that will burn that Washington squirrel cage down unless
men returning from the war get their just desserts."

Of course, the letter writer's question was rhetorical. Most of
the nation knew that Atherton, who had served under General
Pershing in France during World War I, was the National Commander of the American Legion. And as the head of that veterans'

group, Atherton was both the author and chief lobbyist of a revolutionary bill that would provide the unique combination of a free college education and low-interest home and business loans for all American veterans who had spent more than ninety days in uniform.

Yet while the fuming letter writer narrow-mindedly believed that victory would be sufficient "just desserts" for the nation's returning armed forces, Atherton's more enlightened view would ultimately prevail. And the story of how Atherton's persistence mobilized the country, President Franklin Roosevelt, and Congress to enact the G.I. Bill (Servicemen's Readjustment Act of 1944) is one more illustration of how a strong-willed individual can persuade government to use its money and authority creatively to build a better America.

The G.I. Bill was a landmark law whose important benefits to the nation can be measured in the quantifiable revenues that accompany new jobs, new construction of homes, and new tax proceeds. But, no less significant, it was also legislation that in many incalculable ways changed the fabric and spirit of American life. The G.I. Bill made the country better educated, more egalitarian, and more optimistic, a land where the prospect of opportunity lifted and energized the citizenry.

AS I LEARNED FIRSTHAND.

When I returned to Middlebury College, a small liberal arts institution near Lake Champlain in Vermont, for the fall semester in 1946, two new students were assigned to my room. They were older than my previous roommates, but that was not the only difference. They came to Middlebury after serving in the military, would not have been able to attend without government assistance, and they brought with them a seriousness of purpose that was rare among undergraduates. Yet there was also, as I would quickly come to discover, something else about these veterans turned freshmen.

At the time, we were living in a fraternity house. One fall afternoon, a stern-faced representative from the national headquarters of our fraternity arrived to threaten our chapter with expulsion. The reason was that there were two "unsuitable" members in the house. One was African-American; the other was Jewish.

That was me. My family and I had come to America in 1942 after escaping from Nazi-occupied France. We had made our tense, often frightened way to North Africa, then on to Portugal, then Brazil, until, as luck would have it, we arrived in the United States. Only now I was informed I must leave my home in a bucolic American college town for the same reason my parents had been forced to flee our house in France: my Jewishness.

The representative from the national chapter explained there was "nothing personal" in his demanding the resignation of the two offending members. "Some of my best friends are Jewish," he insisted to me with an improbable sincerity.

I was angry. I was scared. And I didn't see any alternative to being forced once again to move on.

Then the two veterans intervened. Politely yet forcefully, they explained to the visitor that they had not fought a war against the Nazis in Europe to see racial laws enacted in the United States.

With the shocked national representative wedged stiffly between them, the two veterans escorted the man out of the house and to the railroad station.

I was in awe. In all my family's hectic flight across the world, I had never encountered anyone who had stood up for Jews (or, for that matter, blacks). After all my grim experiences, I had never expected I would. Yet those two veterans demonstrated to me and my classmates that in postwar America a new, more egalitarian future was possible.

Shortly after that incident, our chapter was expelled from the national fraternity. Nevertheless, we continued to rent the house. It was a remarkable experience. What I learned over the next two years from the veterans who shared my living quarters and my classrooms expanded my world of ideas and experiences, as at the same time I grew to appreciate my newly adopted country: a land of opportunities.

Although this is a personal tale—and an admittedly small one—its implications, are both illustrative and heuristic. For it was this and other incidents at colleges and universities throughout the country that demonstrated the unique transformative power of the G.I. Bill. Mine is but one little example of the large, unexpected (and often even unarticulated) dividends a wise and visionary investment can bring to American life.

EVEN BEFORE WARREN ATHERTON began his determined public campaign, there had been a history of the government's instituting programs to reward its veterans—but those benefits were poorly administered and went only to the wounded and the disabled.

Veterans of the War of 1812 and the Mexican War, for example, were awarded small pensions if they had been shot or had suffered disabling injuries in combat. In 1818, veterans of the Revolutionary War were retroactively awarded pensions if they had served for at least two years and were either disabled or insolvent.

But the scale, the ferocity, and the carnage of World War I compelled Congress to reevaluate what it owed those who had gone off to war. Five million Americans served in "the Great War." Approximately 117,000 soldiers were killed; 200,000 were wounded. Legislators and the president decided that it was proper and just to try to repay the terrible sacrifices made by all who had served—not only those who had had been wounded or disabled.

Legislation was passed that gave every discharged World War I veteran $60, a train ticket home, and the guarantee of a $500 bonus to be paid in 1944. The Bonus Act also provided for a twenty-year endowment against which a veteran could borrow.

But while the bonus legislation had been conceived by a grateful Congress and had been cheered by the returning soldiers in 1919, neither the legislators nor the veterans had anticipated the economic upheavals that would rock the nation a decade later. In 1929, the stock market crashed, and the Great Depression soon gripped the country. Many of the doughboy heroes of the Great War found themselves, like millions of Americans, without jobs, forced each day to go to soup kitchens and stand on breadlines.

Destitute, these veterans insisted they could not wait until 1944 to receive their pledged bonus. They needed it now! In 1932, as we have seen, 20,000 desperate veterans from all over the country organized a "Bonus March" on Washington to demand an early payment of the promised $500. After violence erupted, the U.S.

Army's intervention was a disaster. General Douglas MacArthur's guns and tanks were turned on his own veterans. It was a heartless, disproportionate response to men who had made sacrifices for the nation, and it deeply shook America.

Nine years later, in 1941, as the nation went off to a new war and the first peacetime draft in American history had been instituted, the memory of the sad circumstances that had pushed the veteran doughboys to violence and despair remained strong. Furthermore, World War II was a conflict that engaged the nation to a previously unimaginable extent. By the end of the fighting, nearly 16 million American men and women were in uniform— 11 million in the Army, 4 million in the Navy, and 600,000 in the Marines. In addition, 350,000 women voluntarily served in support activities. More than 400,000 soldiers would be killed; 600,000 wounded.

Yet the all-out effort that had defeated the Axis powers also resulted in another victory. America was now fully employed, the nation a giant factory where there was work for everyone; and the Great Depression finally came to an end. This newfound prosperity left many legislators and President Roosevelt confident that the returning soldiers would be able to integrate themselves successfully into a booming peacetime economy.

Eleanor Roosevelt, in her nationally syndicated newspaper columns, was not as sanguine as her husband. Throughout the war, she continually urged the passage of legislation to provide benefits for the returning troops. President Roosevelt, however, was less concerned. In a 1943 speech to the American Legion, he sternly warned, "No person, because he wore a uniform, must thereafter be placed in a special class of beneficiaries over all and other citizens."

As the war raged on, Roosevelt and his advisers gave relatively little practical thought to what would happen to the 16 million men and women who would return to their homes once the hostilities ceased. Understandably, the president was more concerned with winning the war than with the consequences of a still distant peace.

IN 1939, BEFORE AMERICA entered the war, Roosevelt had created the National Resources Planning Board (NRPB). Its purpose was to plan for the future management of national resources. Once the country went to war, the president decided that rather than empower a new agency to deal with the anticipated problems associated with bringing millions of returning veterans back into postwar life, the NRPB should include this, too, in its broad mandate.

Frederick A. Delano, the president's uncle, headed the NRPB, and he studiously began to focus on the issues involved in the demobilization of a massive army. He released a series of reports that provided a detailed, if somewhat wishful, plan to boost the economy by drawing down postwar unemployment to zero. And that was just for starters. The NRPB announced that it also wanted to create a "New Bill of Rights" for all citizens, not just those affected by service in the war.

The president, a busy wartime commander in chief, was taken aback by the agency's ambitions. "This is no time," Roosevelt reprimanded, "for a public interest in or discussion of the post-war problems on the broad ground that there will not be any post-war problems if we lose this war." As a more realistic compromise, the president instead agreed to a "wholly unpublicized off-the-record examination" of possible programs that could help those who had left their normal lives and jobs to serve.

A new committee, the Postwar Readjustments of the Civilian and Military Personnel (PMC), was established to conduct this "off-the-record" investigation. It was technically under the authority of Delano and the NRPB, but it functioned as an independent body. Comprised mostly of fiscal conservatives who were specialists in education, from the start the PMC understood that its recommendations were to be limited in scope, nothing like the sweeping proposals issued by the NRPB.

In the end, its report to the president reflected this constrained mandate. It modestly suggested that returning veterans receive merit-based education and training for one year; three-month military severance pay; and unemployment benefits for up to six months as long as they were claimed within a year of a soldier's demobilization.

These were recommendations that in their narrow way seemed to reflect the spirit of the president's assignment. And their appearance was well timed. Only days before he received the report, Roosevelt had announced: "We are laying plans for the return to civilian life of our gallant men and women in the armed services. They must not be demobilized into an environment of inflation and unemployment to a place on a bread line or on a corner selling apples."

However, when the president commented on the PMC report

in 1943, his support was carefully guarded. Roosevelt conceded that he agreed with its general ideas; nevertheless, he declined to endorse any of its specific proposals.

A large part of the president's reluctance was not philosophical but rather an acknowledgment of the political realities. While public opinion polls showed that nearly 90 percent of Americans felt returning soldiers should be "given a chance to get back to school at the government's expense," Congress was unenthusiastic. And the editorials that appeared regularly in newspapers throughout the country were even less supportive, many of them blatantly vitriolic in their opposition to veterans' benefits.

When Congress, angry that the topic of veterans' benefits was scheduled for debate, voted to cut off further funding for the NRPB, Roosevelt, with his customary practicality, understood the situation. Now was not the propitious time to put forward a plan for America's returning soldiers.

BUT EVEN AS THE president waited for the correct political moment to take action, his heart and mind were already committed. Two years earlier, in his lyrical 1941 State of the Union address—the famous "Four Freedoms" speech—Roosevelt was quite clear. He did not mention veterans, but he did articulate a benevolent and democratic vision for a postwar America:

> *There is nothing mysterious about the foundations of a healthy and strong democracy. The basic things expected by our people of their political and economic systems are simple. They are: Equality of opportunity for youth and others.*

Jobs for those who can work. Security for those who need it. The ending of special privilege for the few. The preservation of civil liberties for all.

In late 1942, as the president signed an amendment to the Selective Service Act of 1918 lowering the draft age to eighteen, he also announced the formation of a new committee. The Armed Forces Committee on Postwar Educational Opportunities for Service Personnel would at last try to translate Roosevelt's staunchly egalitarian and moralistic concepts into a practical legislative veterans' program.

Chaired by Brigadier General Frederick Osborn, the group quickly became known as the Osborn Committee. Its primary task was to help young men whose education had been interrupted by military service resume their schooling, and to offer other veterans opportunities for training and education when they returned from the war. In a message to Congress supporting the committee, Roosevelt pointedly endorsed its lofty purpose. "Lack of money," the president insisted, "should not prevent any veteran of this war from equipping himself for the most useful employment for which his attitude and willingness prepare him." He then went on to outline several specific recommendations to the committee.

The Osborn Committee's final recommendations, however, aspired to significantly less than appeared to be endorsed by the president's uncompromising words. They included, for example, the suggestion that all who served for at least six months should receive a year of education. But the committee categorically restricted the total of those who would be eligible for more than a year's tuition to a mere 100,000 veterans—out of a service force of nearly 16 million American men and women.

On October 27, 1943, Roosevelt sent Congress the Osborn Committee's recommendations. Along with other limited benefits proposals, the entire disappointing package was incorporated into a veterans' bill introduced by Senator Elbert D. Thomas, a Utah Democrat.

Few substantive benefits were offered in the Thomas bill. Its provisions clearly fell way short of the essential democratic goals Roosevelt had eloquently articulated in his 1941 State of the Union. Yet it was, apparently, the most that returning soldiers could realistically hope for.

BUT THEN WARREN ATHERTON and the American Legion took up the cause.

Established in the aftermath of World War I, the American Legion was chartered by Congress in 1919 as "a patriotic, mutual-help, war-time veterans organization." At its twenty-fifth annual convention in September 1943, as the fighting continued without any prospect of an end in Europe and the Pacific, the Legion nevertheless began to think about what would happen when the war was over. A special committee was formed to assist veterans with rehabilitation following discharge. Serving as chairman was the Legion's National Commander, Warren Atherton.

Atherton had no formal higher education, and was just a clerk in a Stockton, California, law office when he went off to fight in World War I. Upon his return from France, however, he married the daughter of the founder of the Caterpillar Tractor Company and managed to get himself admitted to the California bar. Although largely self-taught, Atherton had a facile, often inventive mind, and he brought a crusader's passion to many of the cases he represented. Fueled by his own experiences in the Great War, dismayed by the still strong memory of a Bonus Army of ragged veterans trying to get token recognition of their service, empowered by his position in the Legion, Atherton threw himself with all his zeal and passion into the World War II veterans' cause.

He did not support onetime bonuses, but rather wanted veterans to get, as his fellow committee member Harry Colmery put it, "a square deal." Atherton's concept of a benefit package was pervasive: its goal was to integrate the citizen-soldier upon his return into the rush of twentieth-century American life.

The American Legion special committee convened in Washington on December 15, 1943, to discuss the specifics of what needed to be done. Goaded on by Atherton's passionate commitment, in an energetic three weeks the committee crafted a first draft of what would become the G.I. Bill.

This remarkable document offered four revolutionary benefits that would be available to any World War II veteran who was not dishonorably discharged and who had served at least ninety days after September 16, 1940:

One: "The opportunity of resuming education or technical training after discharge, or taking a refresher or retrainer course," for which the government would pay up to $500 per school year and provide a monthly allowance while the veteran was enrolled.

Two: Vocational education and on-the-job training.

Three: Housing and business loans guaranteed by the federal government.

Four: Unemployment benefits of $20 per week for up to a year, in order to allow for readjustment.

There were also additional provisions crafted to assist veterans in finding jobs, and to provide medical coverage including, if necessary, hospitalization. All of these benefits would be available for between one and four years.

In the second week of January 1944, after a meeting in the Oval Office with Atherton, President Roosevelt introduced the bill drafted by the Legion committee to Congress. "This nation is morally obligated to provide this training and education," the president firmly admonished the legislators.

AS THE CONGRESSIONAL DEBATE began, opponents of the bill rushed to Washington to voice their objections. Educators worried that the proposed flood of new students would inevitably lower academic standards at colleges. Unions complained that the new workforce would take their members' jobs. Bankers were anxious about the consequences of mass defaults on federal housing and business loans made to returning soldiers. Other veterans' organizations feared that a widespread distribution of government funds to all who had served would penalize those who most needed assistance—the wounded and the disabled. And there was vociferous opposition from those who did not want to give benefits or opportunities to black veterans despite their wartime service.

But Atherton remained undaunted. He had an instinctive public relations genius, and he used the Legion and its nationwide membership to mount a surprisingly sophisticated grassroots campaign in support of the bill. He shrewdly presented the proposal as "A Bill of Rights for GI Joe and GI Jane," and argued that the right to education, employment, and a home of their own was a debt of honor that the nation owed to those who had gone off to fight to defend the security of all Americans. In the midst of a bitterly fought war, this appeal—patriotic, reasonable, and egalitarian—struck an empathetic chord.

With a relentless determination and a general's command, Atherton marshaled all his available resources. He made himself available to the press and to Congress. He appeared on radio and in film clips. He made sure every Legion post in the country sent a petition with a long list of signatures to Congress urging passage of the bill. And arguably most consequential of all his efforts, he convinced the publishing magnate William Randolph Hearst to support the legislation. Hearst had originally opposed America's entry into the war; but coaxed on by Atherton, the publisher now made sure his nationwide chain of newspapers were solidly behind the G.I. Bill.

As the public's support for veterans' benefits grew, Congress began to take notice. On March 24, 1944, the Senate passed the law by a 50–0 vote. In the House, a slightly different version of the bill was bottled up in committee, but it finally moved forward on May 18 with another unanimous vote, 387–0. Now only one legislative hurdle remained: a joint House-Senate conference committee had to resolve the small differences in the two versions of the bill.

After three weeks of debate, the seven-member committee

voted on the newly recast bill. The vote was 3 to 3. The one remaining, deciding vote belonged to Representative John Gibson of Georgia. However, he had returned to Georgia, leaving his proxy vote in support of the bill with the committee's chairman, Representative John Rankin. Only now Rankin, a Mississippi segregationist who opposed the bill's provision granting unemployment insurance to all veterans regardless of the color of their skin, refused to cast Gibson's favorable vote.

It was Friday, June 9, just three days after D-Day in Normandy, and the vote was scheduled for the next morning at ten. If the deadlock remained, the bill would die in committee. The only hope was if Gibson would appear to cast his own tie-breaking vote. But where was Gibson? In less than twenty-four hours he needed to be found and brought to the House floor.

All that his office knew was that the congressman was somewhere near his home in southern Georgia. Rural telephone operators began calling frantically around the state. Atherton persuaded the *Atlanta Constitution* to join the hunt, and the newspaper in turn enlisted the help of the state police. Meanwhile, Legion officials arranged for an army plane to be standing by, ready to fly Gibson back to Washington.

At eleven o'clock on Friday night, Gibson was at last found. He was rushed to the Army base and the waiting plane. Except now the plane proved to be inoperable.

All appeared lost. There was no way to get to Washington in time for the vote. Then a commercial flight leaving Jacksonville, Florida, at 2:25 Saturday morning was discovered. Would the congressman be able to get to the airport in time?

Escorted by a procession of state troopers on motorcycles,

lights flashing, Gibson's car sped at 90 miles per hour through the night on its way to the airport. He made it.

Gibson arrived on the House floor just in time to cast the deciding vote. But before he voted yes, he reminded his colleagues why the bill was necessary. As we sit in Washington, he told them, American servicemen are fighting their way through France and on to Germany. We owe them for their service.

On June 22, 1944, President Franklin Roosevelt signed the Servicemen's Readjustment Act of 1944.

NO ONE WILL WORK, critics of the bill had ranted. Why should they? The returning soldiers will simply cash their guaranteed $20 weekly unemployment/readjustment pay. It will create a crippling drain on the federal government.

But this was not the case. Only one out of every nineteen veterans received the full fifty-two weeks of checks. Less than one fifth of the potential unemployment benefits the federal Treasury might have paid were claimed. Instead, the veterans took full advantage of the bill's educational benefits.

Educators had been concerned about the bill's impact, worrying that a deluge of allegedly academically unprepared students would cause college standards to deteriorate. "Educational hobo jungles"—that was the predicated fate of American institutions once the stream of rowdy veterans arrived, according to Robert Hutchings, the respected president of the University of Chicago. Hutchings and the other critics, however, were proved wrong. Throughout the country, institutions reacted favorably to the ability and commitment of the veterans turned students. A study by *Fortune* found that the postwar class of 1949 was "the best . . . the most mature . . . the most responsible, the most self-disciplined group of college students in history."

The veterans enrolled in U.S. schools in an unanticipated number. In 1940, only 160,000 people earned college degrees; by 1947, there were 1,164,000 students enrolled in institutions of higher education—and 49 percent, more than a half-million men and women, were veterans.

The G.I. Bill made higher education a basic part of American life. And it helped to change the institutions. Catholics, Jews, and blacks were admitted in significant numbers for the first time to many colleges. Women and married students with children also were, thanks to the G.I. Bill, given the opportunity to pursue a college degree.

By the end of the program, in 1956, out of a veteran population of over 15.4 million, more than half—about 7.8 million individuals—participated in either traditional educational or vocational programs. The specific enrollment numbers would no doubt have pleased Warren Atherton: 2.23 million went to college; 3.48 million received other education, including high school diploma equivalency programs; 1.4 million signed on for on-the-job training; and 690,000 benefited from farm training programs.

The total cost of the World War II federally funded education program was $14.5 billion. Yet the return on that colossal investment was nothing less than the creation of a knowledge-driven America—the society that provided the economic engine for the second half of the twentieth century.

• • •

NO LESS IMPORTANT THAN the bill's educational benefits to the country were its unprecedented home, business, and farm loan provisions. A total of 29 percent of all returning veterans—about 5 million Americans—participated in these programs.

Consider housing: The depression and material shortages during the war had created an enormous housing shortage. In September 1946, a *Time* magazine article despairingly entitled "No Place to Live" reported that the lack of homes was "a national problem as serious and compelling as the war itself." Discharged veterans were getting married in record numbers across the nation—only too many of these new families had no place to live.

The G.I. Bill changed this grim situation, and enabled millions of Americans to become homeowners. The mortgage rate was set at an economical 4 percent and the federally backed Veterans Association (VA) guaranteed up to 50 percent of the entire loan.

The VA-guaranteed loans were not only for houses. Farms and businesses were also funded under provisions of the G.I. Bill.

The injection of these federal funds into the economy sent it booming. House construction soared, and the building trades prospered. The suburbs grew. A better America, whose families enjoyed a better standard of living, more secure and comfortable in their daily life and their prospects for the future, took shape.

"THE G.I. BILL WAS the best piece of legislation ever passed by the U.S. Congress," wrote the historian Stephen Ambrose. "It made modern America."

It was a landmark investment whose dividends continue to pay off. And it is a model for new Athertons to study, a blueprint for benevolent legislative initiatives and federal capital investments as an America facing new economic and social crises and fighting new wars proceeds into a tumultuous new century.

TEN

The Interstate
Highway System

PARKED JUST SOUTH OF the White House grounds, the Army convoy stretched in a twisting three-mile-long line of cars, trucks, and motorcycles. The engines of the big khaki trucks were festooned with red, white, and blue bunting, and banners on their side panels announced, WE'RE OFF FOR FRISCO." There were speeches from several senators and the secretary of war, and then a fifteen-piece band began to play. Finally, at 11:15 on the morning of July 7, 1919, the order was given: "Move out!" Two hundred and sixty enlisted men and thirty-five officers climbed into their vehicles. Moments later seventy-two engines started in a roar, and the convoy lurched forward.

The U.S. Army's first transcontinental trip had begun. It had been conceived by Captain Bernard McMahon as a way to demonstrate the military capabilities of motor vehicles and, at the same time, to get support for the Army from a seemingly disinterested nation now that World War I was over.

Captain McMahon's inspired plan worked. As the caravan made its slow way west passing through cities and towns, it captivated America. The sixty-two-day journey was celebrated with fireworks, speeches, picnics, and parades. More than 3.5 million people lined the route, cheering on the procession.

Yet as history would come to look back on this adventure, more consequential than the American public's interest in this grueling cross-country trip would be the lasting effect it had on just one of its participants—a young Army lieutenant.

After graduating from West Point, this newly commissioned officer had looked forward to going off to France to fight in "the war to end all wars." The armistice, however, ended these ambitions and his military career had stalled. He signed on for the convoy with the small hope that a new opportunity might somehow revitalize both his listless mood and his future in the Army. There was also another inducement: He was stationed in Fort Benning, Georgia, while his wife and young son were living across the country in Denver. As the convoy headed to the west coast, he hoped he could be reunited, however briefly, with his family.

And so with a sense of anticipation but little enthusiasm, Lieutenant Dwight D. Eisenhower volunteered. The experience was a revelation—a trip, as he would later write, "through darkest America." After the first three days of engine and equipment breakdowns, of driving on "non-existent" roads that were dirt, mud, and sand, the convoy had traveled only 165 miles west of Washington. The entire continent still stretched dauntingly before them. "We were not sure it could be accomplished at all," he remembered.

The procession crept along at a frustrating five miles an hour. There were many days when all they could manage was three miles. Accidents and breakdowns were the norm. In the Sierras, a truck hurdled off a makeshift road and crashed into a ravine. But Eisenhower and the convoy persevered. And when the trucks rolled into North Platte, Nebraska, his wife, Mamie, was holding their young son and waiting to greet him.

By the September morning when the convoy rode in triumphant procession through the streets of San Francisco—Eisenhower would recall in his memoirs—the long and arduous journey "had started me thinking about good, two-lane highways." With the victory in Europe, America had become a world power; yet, as he observed with frustration, "the road system of the United States . . . may have been less usable for transcontinental travel than it had been fifty or sixty years earlier." He was convinced that the nation must be "interested in producing better roads."

More than three decades later, that young lieutenant, now a retired four-star general, was sworn in as the thirty-fourth president of the United States. The memory of his difficult two-month trip across the continent, however, remained strong. The passing years and his experiences as Allied Commander during World War II had only served to reinforce his far-thinking conviction that the nation's welfare, security, and commerce were dependent to a significant degree on the ease of mobility from coast to coast, from north to south. And now President Eisenhower set out to use the power of his office to sponsor the extraordinary federal legislation that would connect the country in a vast interlocking series of roads—the Interstate Highway Bill.

THE INTERSTATE HIGHWAY SYSTEM is, in part, the story of the construction of America's vital core infrastructure, the creation of the longest and most extensive engineered roadway in history.

We have always been a people on the move. The American Experience is grounded in the optimistic belief that this is a big country with new opportunities out there for those who are willing to find them. In many ways, the history of this country is the story of people who decided to move on: to cross a distant hill, to ford another river, to travel to the next town.

And so from the nation's founding there have been attempts to build thoroughfares that would connect one part of the country to another. Daniel Boone and other intrepid pioneers had blazed the Cumberland Pike, and in the early 1800s there was a movement to build a National Road along this well-worn route stretching from Cumberland, Maryland, to Vandalia, Illinois. The first segment of this proudly National Road was financed in a provision of the 1803 legislation that admitted Ohio into the Union. Opening in 1818, it connected Cumberland to Wheeling, West Virginia (Wheeling was then part of Virginia), and was from the start heavily trafficked.

But despite the hopes of its promoters, the National Road was never completed. From its inception, it was mired in controversy. Congressional opponents argued that the original idea for financing further construction with federal tolls was unconstitutional, and Presidents Van Buren and Tyler, both fiercely strict constructionists, agreed. They vetoed appropriations to extend the route. With no support forthcoming from the federal government, the once enticing prospect of a National Road quietly died. In 1836, the deteriorating roadway was ceded back to the individual states that it passed through.

Yet even as the reality of a National Road came to a political dead end, the idea of a transportation system that would connect the far corners of the country continued to attract fellow travelers. Only now the vision was modified: the country would be united not by highways but rather by railroad lines.

From the Civil War until 1918, 254,000 miles of track were laid across America. In the often challenging hands-on process, engineers learned a great deal about geology, drainage, and blasting. This hard-won knowledge would prove to be invaluable once a quickly infatuated nation began to appreciate the potential in high-speed automobile motoring—and America at last became serious about road construction.

IT WAS AN UNPRECEDENTED—and astonishing—feat. In 1901, a twenty-one-year-old mechanic, Roy Chapin, did the seemingly impossible. He had set out to drive from Detroit to New York City in a $650 Oldsmobile. Nine days after his departure, a mud-covered Chapin walked into the Broadway hotel hosting the New

York Automobile Show and announced his accomplishment. When news of his successful journey was reported in banner headlines in newspapers throughout the country, for the first time Americans began to appreciate fully how automobiles might change their lives.

But even with his triumph, Chapin realized that cars would only be valuable if there were roads on which they could drive. He went on to become president of the Hudson Motor Company and then teamed up with Carl G. Fisher to promote a resourceful scheme. Fisher, the owner of an Indianapolis headlight manufacturing company, wanted the early automobile makers to finance a New York–to–San Francisco highway.

Both Fisher and Chapin pointed out the economic logic in their plan: though it would cost the car manufacturers capital to build the road, they would reap a significant return on this investment from the sale of vehicles to the people who would travel the roadway. Nevertheless, Henry Ford, the leading car manufacturer, was not persuaded. Regardless of the potential economic benefits, he objected in principle to private citizens' funding a construction project that was, he insisted, the responsibility of the federal government. Without his support, the plan for a privately capitalized cross-country roadway appeared to have little chance of moving forward.

Fisher and Chapin, however, were determined. They brazenly decided to ignore Ford's objections and went on to form the Lincoln Highway Association. The association succeeded in convincing a large number of private individuals and community groups to build "seedling miles" in their towns. As a result, all across the country stretches of existing dirt roads were paved. The completed

Lincoln Highway was a hodgepodge affair, a patched-together thoroughfare where newly paved roads would abruptly stop and a treacherously rutted dirt road would suddenly begin. But it did encourage an automobile-crazed nation's growing dream of transcontinental motoring. And, no less significant, it helped to goad the energies and imaginations of previously reluctant federal legislators.

INSPIRED BY THE EXAMPLE of the Lincoln Highway, Congress in 1912 passed the Post Road Act. This legislation helped to fund highway building in several states and also established the precedent of state oversight of these federally funded construction projects.

Four years later, in 1916, the principle of federal-state cooperation in road building was further reinforced with the passage of the Federal Aid Road Act. This bill specified that state highway departments would receive the government funds. Thereafter, while federal dollars paid for the construction projects, the states controlled the design and building of the roads within their borders.

This very practical federal-state arrangement would remain in place for the next forty years and would work successfully enough to build a 200,000-mile network of roads. And throughout this long period of fruitful cooperation, two powerful organizations that were already in existence when the 1916 Road Act became law guided and controlled the intragovernmental process.

One was the American Association of State Highway Officials (AASHO). Organized in 1914 by state highway commissioners and engineers to discuss legislative, financial, and technical issues, AASHO was able to collect the many and varied facts necessary to determine the best (that is, the least expensive and/or politically viable) routes through the states. Its information proved so authoritative that in time its power expanded: officials in Washington would allow the states to choose where the federally funded roads would go—as long as AASHO approved.

The second organization, the Bureau of Public Roads (BPR), originally created in 1903 as the Office of Road Inquiry, controlled the federal role in road construction. From 1919 to 1953, Thomas MacDonald, the former chief engineer of the Iowa Highway Commission, led the BPR, and he proved to be a particularly shrewd and manipulative powerbroker.

In his first speech as BPR commissioner, MacDonald spoke out against the building of national highways simply to facilitate interstate travel. He argued that intrastate roadways should be built to serve more purposeful pursuits; for example, to make it easier for farmers to move crops and livestock to markets. This practical approach to road building became the federal standard under MacDonald's draconian leadership of the BPR. For more than three decades, neither presidents nor governors would consider launching a road construction project without first obtaining MacDonald's approval. It was an almost dictatorial process, but it also served to institutionalize further the remarkable federal-state partnership in highway construction.

BY THE 1920S, AMERICA'S love affair with automobiles had turned into a big business—and one with the happy prospects of growing even bigger. The promise of hundreds of thousands of cars speeding down the nation's roads excited an influential coalition: automakers, cement, asphalt, and steel producers, petroleum companies, road contractors, insurance companies, banks, even hotel operators. If cars were to be the future of American life, then roads would be needed—and in the process, fortunes would be made for many citizens. By the mid-twentieth century, one in every six Americans, however tangentially, would earn his or her living from the automobile and associated industries.

It was a potentially powerful lobby; but it was not a unified force. The trucking industry, the American Automobile Association, the construction unions—each segment of the "highway lobby" petitioned Congress with its own specific and sometimes contradictory demands.

This fragmented approach resulted in a frustratingly mercurial response by legislators. In 1921, for example, Congress passed a potentially landmark bill that called for the linking of all counties in the nation by paved roads. Yet despite the bill's visionary aspirations, it resulted in relatively little actual road construction.

Even President Franklin Roosevelt, whose personal force and canny political maneuverings (as we have seen) were able to guide dozens of revolutionary New Deal programs through Congress, could not win support for a transcontinental road system. He tried on two separate occasions to get a nationwide highway construction bill through the House and the Senate, and each time he failed.

So Roosevelt, with a politician's easy practicality, simply scaled down his proposal. Now the president put his energies and imprimatur behind a smaller project, but one that he hoped would nevertheless demonstrate to the American people the economic and cultural benefits of large-scale road building. He proposed the Pennsylvania Turnpike to Congress.

From the start, Thomas MacDonald opposed the project. According to the adamant BPR chairman, it did not matter if the road was built with public or private monies. "No one would use it," he predicted. But Roosevelt was certain MacDonald was wrong. He challenged the chairman with what was a very persuasive argument in the midst of the Great Depression: building the turnpike would create badly needed jobs. This logic made sense to Congress, and for once MacDonald was overruled. Federal funding for the Pennsylvania Turnpike was approved.

The nation's first superhighway was built using land that had been partially cleared and tunnels that were originally dug to be part of William Vanderbilt and Andrew Carnegie's South Pennsylvania Railroad. This line had been meant to challenge the Pennsylvania Railroad's monopoly on service in that part of the country, but was eventually abandoned. Now the cleared route was inventively put to another use. The years of previous work enabled the turnpike to be built much faster than its critics—including MacDonald—had anticipated. The highway opened in 1938, charging a toll of $1.50 per vehicle, and was an immediate success.

Yet even before the road had been completed, Roosevelt was certain of the economic and strategic benefits that would accompany a large interstate highway system. Under the national Industrial Recovery Act, the New Deal already employed a half-million people building roads through funding that was funneled through state highway departments. FDR wanted to create even more jobs with road construction funding that would flow directly from the federal Treasury. His model for this program was in many ways inspired by the extensive high-speed Autobahns Hitler had built for military and commercial transportation across Germany.

According to Roosevelt's plan, the federal government would set up a public corporation to build "ten self-sustaining, transcontinental highways as a national defense and business pump-priming measure."

But even with the apparent success of the Pennsylvania Turnpike, Roosevelt knew he would still need to enlist MacDonald's support for a larger highway plan. This time, his strategy was not to try persuade the BPR chief; rather, he would use the power of his office to issue commands.

In 1937, the president met with a stone-faced MacDonald and announced that he was officially putting him in charge of a program to construct a network of transcontinental highways. From the start, Roosevelt set out to control the meeting. On a map of the United States, the president authoritatively drew three lines east-to-west and three more north-to-south. These were the routes, the president sternly ordered, where he wanted the highways built. He explained that the federal government would purchase two-mile-wide strips of land where the roads would run, and sell the unused acreage to home developers. New communities, he predicted, would quickly spring up around the interstate highway lines. Additional revenues would be earned by charging tolls. According to Roosevelt's confidently optimistic scenario, the highway toll revenues would eventually pay off the construction costs.

MacDonald listened respectfully, but left the meeting determined to put all his energy and personal power into opposing the president's project. He was convinced that people would not use the system; it was a vast and expensive construction project that would have no practical use. And his pragmatic complaint was further supported by a philosophical one: He vehemently opposed toll roads, believing the concept was unconstitutional. But there was also another important factor that put iron into his resolve. MacDonald didn't like being ordered about by anyone, including the president of the United States.

Insulted, MacDonald went to war. He wrote a long and detailed denunciation of Roosevelt's plan. And then he held a series of meetings with key congressmen, all indebted to him for his previous support for road construction in their states, to voice personally his many objections.

Even before the MacDonald report was submitted to Congress, the president knew he was beaten. There were only so many political battles he could fight. An economic depression and a world war were consuming enough challenges. Roosevelt doubted he could find either the will or the political ingenuity to confront the stubborn and well-connected BPR chairman and win. He had built the Pennsylvania Turnpike and that would have to suffice. With a shrug of philosophical resignation, Roosevelt abandoned his plans for a national highway system.

• • •

BY THE TIME DWIGHT D. Eisenhower was sworn in as the nation's thirty-fourth president in January 1953, America was a radically different nation. The new president anticipated that he would have a much more receptive audience for any proposal to build highways.

After all, millions of families now owned cars. Further, thousands of miles of roads had already been built throughout the United States that could serve as models for a system of divided traffic highways. Conveying people in and out of New York City, for example, were the Henry Hudson and Bronx River parkways, as well as Connecticut's winding scenic Merritt Parkway. Across the country in Los Angeles, the Arroyo Seco Parkway was another well-functioning and well-used roadway. Further, many sophisticatedly engineered bridge and tunnel projects had already been successfully built, including the Golden Gate Bridge in San Francisco, the George Washington Bridge over the Hudson River, and the Holland and Lincoln tunnels connecting New York City and New Jersey.

Additionally, the nation could now rely on the skills of a new generation of well-trained engineers. Military engineers had returned from World War II, studied road construction under the G.I. Bill, and then gone off to work for state highway departments. They would be prepared for the technological challenge of a vast interstate highway system.

Eisenhower's own military experience had also convinced him that postwar America would be persuaded if a case were made for the strategic importance of highways. In World War II, the Allies had persistently rained down bombs on the German roadways, but despite the craters, Eisenhower had noted, the enemy supply convoys managed to get through. And now that the United States was locked in a Cold War, a high-speed road system provided an additional strategic benefit. Highways would be the best way to evacuate American cities if Soviet nuclear missiles were launched.

Even the federal and state agencies that had for decades opposed a national highway system had helped to prepare the way for Eisenhower's vision. There now were uniform design and construction standards for all state roads. Over the years, road-building materials and techniques had been exhaustively tested. The necessary technological and engineering groundwork had been completed, and the results were widely approved and accepted.

Still, Eisenhower, a political realist, realized that the opposition to a federal highway system was both influential and well entrenched. MacDonald's BPR and the AASHO would continue to fight any plans for a cross-country road system. And the state highway departments would join in, fighting any federal attempt to take over road construction. The prospect of the states' losing thousands of patronage jobs as well as control over the distribution of construction monies would undoubtedly lead to an intense battle in Congress.

Nevertheless, Eisenhower decided that he would move forward. The nation needed an interstate highway system.

THE PRESIDENT HAD CHOSEN his moment carefully. He had decided to announce his great plan in a setting where he felt it would attract the attention of both politicians and the American people.

He would lay out his proposal for what would be the most massive engineering project since the Great Pyramids in a speech in July 1954 to the National Governors Association, which was meeting in Lake George, New York.

But Eisenhower never made it to Lake George. His sister-in-law had died and he felt he must attend her funeral. In his place he sent his vice president, Richard Nixon, to appear at the governors' conference.

Holding Eisenhower's notes, glancing at them one final time, Nixon went with some trepidation to the podium. But the speech the vice president delivered did not seem as if he were simply mouthing another man's words. He spoke with passion and commitment.

Nixon began by sharing Eisenhower's experience on the truck convoy across America thirty-five years earlier—a journey, he told the enthralled governors, that "had taken sixty days and 6,000 breakdowns." Then he went on to present a grand plan that "solves the problem of speedy, safe transcontinental travel" for a country where seven out of ten families owned a car. It would be a highway system that would unite the nation and at the same time end "an annual death toll" on American roads that was "comparable to the casualties of a bloody war." It would also continue the long-running federal-state partnership in road building, leaving the local governments in charge of their highways.

It was a program, Nixon conceded with daring candor, that would come at an unprecedented price. The cost of an interstate highway program would be $50 billion—and this at a time when the entire annual federal budget was $71 billion.

When Nixon finished, the governors rose to their feet and applauded. The next day, favorable reports of the electrifying speech were carried in newspapers throughout the country.

Now that his revolutionary plan had been successfully shared with the nation, Eisenhower conscientiously moved on to the next set of challenges. With a general's instinct for command, he began to lay the political and tactical groundwork necessary to make the interstate highway system a reality.

MOVING FORWARD RAPIDLY, EISENHOWER designated a team of advisers who would oversee the complicated and massive highway program. Sherman Adams, his resourceful chief of staff, would be responsible for supervising the entire $50 billion construction project. Assisting Adams would be Major General John Stewart Bragdon, who served on the president's Council of Economic Advisers, and Francis DuPont, who had replaced the intractable Thomas MacDonald as head of the BPR.

It was a management team of three strong-willed men who, perhaps predictably, each had his own deeply held view of how the program should be administered. Bragdon proposed replacing the BPR with a National Highway Authority run by the secretaries of defense, commerce, and the Treasury; it would build roads financed entirely by tolls. DuPont, who understandably opposed the idea of eliminating the agency he headed, believed that highway spending would boost the national economy, and therefore the federal government should accept the responsibility to finance and control the entire project. While Adams, who had worked amicably with the BPR when he was governor of New Hampshire, proposed a Continental Highway Finance Corporation that would cooperate with the states as the BPR had done.

Eisenhower listened to these three conflicting strategies—and resolved the debate by creating a new advisory group. The president knew what he wanted, and he decided it would be easier to find men who would be supportive rather than battling with Adams, Bragdon, and DuPont.

He formed the President's Advisory Committee on a National Highway and appointed Lucius Clay, an engineer Eisenhower had known since their days together at West Point, to head the group. The other committee members were bankers, engineers, and union officials who were all directly tied to the automobile industry.

The Clay Committee soon announced that it shared Eisenhower's original vision. Roads were "a capital asset," and the nation could dramatically improve its infrastructure and create jobs without raising taxes or increasing the national debt. Toll roads were also unnecessary. The interstates could be effectively funded through the sale of thirty-year bonds.

Now that Eisenhower had received the recommendation he wanted, he formally submitted his proposal. In 1955, he confidently presented Congress with a bill authorizing a $40 billion, 41,000-mile highway construction program, to be financed by federal bonds.

THE BILL DIED IN committee. Eisenhower's fellow Republicans had decided that the immensely expensive proposal would increase the federal debt too precipitously.

But the president was tenacious. Rather than give up, he continued to try to persuade Congress. It was a difficult and protracted fight.

In the Senate, Harry Byrd, a Virginia Democrat, had assumed the chairmanship of the Finance Committee and he was vehemently opposed to nearly all federal spending. Eisenhower's highway bond financing proposal, however, particularly rankled the influential senator. "Nothing has been proposed in my 22 years in the Senate that would do more to wreck our fiscal system," he charged. He would only consider a pay-as-you-go system of financing for the interstates.

Democratic senator Albert Gore, Sr., of Tennessee then stepped forward to offer his own compromise plan. The BPR, Gore proposed, would spend $10 billion over the next ten years for highway construction, with the federal government putting up 75 percent of the funding and the states the remaining 25 percent. The details of how the plan would be financed were not offered—a coyly deliberate omission that effectively put an end to any debate on the issuing of government bonds. The Senate passed the Gore proposal.

In the House, Maryland Democrat George Fallon, the popular chairman of the Committee on Public Works, introduced his own version of the Gore bill. His legislation extended Gore's proposal until 1968, created a highway trust fund that collected increased gasoline and diesel fuel taxes, and also raised taxes on trucks, tires, and equipment. To placate Senator Byrd, Fallon cannily called his proposal "the pay-as-you-go bill." In a spirit of compromise and resignation, Eisenhower then informed Republican leaders he would abandon his bond financing scheme. They were told to support the Democrat's proposal.

In April 1956, the House passed the Fallon bill by an overwhelming vote of 388 to 19. Senator Gore then reintroduced his legislation, and with its swift approval, the debate began on a compromise conference bill.

The new legislation that emerged from the conference committee contained overly generous funding provisions for cities and made sure the BPR's influence would continue; nevertheless, it was a landmark bill. It authorized $25 billion for twelve years' construction of a National System of Interstate and Defense Highways that were designed, in part, to move military equipment and personnel. It created the Highway Trust Fund, which would be capitalized by an increase in fuel taxes, and at the same time it set the federal contribution to interstate construction at 90 percent. Additionally, the bill authorized right-of-way acquisition of land and set federal construction standards. The entire highway program, the bill optimistically announced, would be completed by 1972.

On June 29, 1956, Eisenhower, recovering from surgery for ileitis, sat in his room at the Walter Reed Hospital and signed the Federal-Aid Highway Act of 1956 into law. It had taken thirty-seven years, but the young lieutenant's vision of an America connected by a network of smoothly paved high-speed roads could finally begin to be realized.

"IMAGINE THE STATE OF Connecticut knee deep in earth; that's how much was moved for the Interstates. Or a wide sidewalk extending from the earth to a point in space five times the distance to the moon; that's how much concrete was poured for the Interstates. Or a land mass the size of the state of Delaware; that's how much property authorities acquired in order to site the Interstates. Or enough drainage culverts to handle all the needs of a city six times the size of Chicago; that's how much was laid beneath the Interstates," wrote Tom Lewis in his compelling account of the building of the highway system, *Divided Highways*.

It was a monumental construction project, an engineering feat that went on for forty years rather than the thirteen that was promised in the original legislation. And there were consequences Eisenhower had not foreseen. The new highways wantonly destroyed urban neighborhoods and downtown centers, encouraged traffic congestion, polluted the air, and helped to institutionalize America's impractical dependence on foreign oil. Yet there is no doubt the Interstate Highway System also played a vital role in creating a new and better America.

Safe and readily accessible roads for high-speed automobile travel led to a building boom that revitalized the economy. Suburbs took shape, and a whole new prosperous and comfortable way of life was inaugurated for millions of Americans. New sectors of industry and commerce appeared—fast-food chains, gas stations, hotels and motels, and repair, financing, and insurance concerns to service the automobile industry. America became a different land. A nation where many routinely drive to work and a land where many are still energized by the prospect of driving off into the sunset.

"The interstate should be a journey, not a destination," Eisenhower hoped. It was a poetic, even spiritual wish. Yet in the end, it was not simply his dream but also a president's sense of commitment that changed America. It was bold and tenacious leadership that led the nation to make the colossal investment in its infrastructure that ultimately made the journey possible.

EPILOGUE

Reading history, I've always believed, begins a dialogue between the past and the present. The events we relive, the battles we fight once again, the disasters we suffer vicariously, the heroes we revere—all guide us through the times in which we live. Looking back can teach us how to engage the world around us.

In the preceding pages, I have shared ten episodes from very different eras in American history. I have chosen these specific case studies because, despite the variety of time and circumstances, each at its core establishes and reinforces similar truths: They illustrate how bold national investments by tenacious leaders helped to create a better America. Together, these stories form a narrative which demonstrates that, contrary to the glib reaction from many contemporary ideological naysayers, large-scale public investments *can* work, and with remarkable long-term success. America, these slices of history show, was built generation after generation by leaders who had a vision of a more secure, more prosperous, more inclusive republic—and who inventively employed the power and resources of the federal government to realize their transformative ideals.

I have told these stories as a person who loves history and believes in its instructive value. Both individually and as a whole, these case studies suggest a response to a crisis that threatens to do no less than undermine the prosperity and security of American life. And I have chosen to tell them because it is imperative today to reaffirm the activist tradition of public investment.

When I first conceived of this book, I was focused on the dangers to America's future caused by a rapidly deteriorating infrastructure and a paucity of investment replaced by speculation. I was, I concede, not prescient enough to predict the totality of the financial crisis—the biggest national economic trauma since the Great Depression—that would occur because of the collapse of the country's housing industry, a crisis in the auto industry, and feverish speculation in the securities markets.

As the preceding chapters demonstrate, America's ascendancy in the world was facilitated by leaders who invested money to build a country that worked. Canals, railroads, highways, schools, electrical power grids—it was this extensive and innovative infrastructure that made life in the United States more comfortable, more egalitarian, and more secure. This reassuring certainty regarding daily life provided successive generations with the solid footing to confront the challenges of their times.

American history shows that economic growth, the creation of wealth, employment, and opportunity, are all built on the
platform of investment. Since Alexander Hamilton, progressive
economic thinkers have followed this path by balancing the participation of both the private and public sectors. However, in recent decades, a new creed of "finance capitalism" has distracted us
from this approach. A radical laissez-faire mind-set credits private
markets with all good economic outcomes and sees the government as no more than a source of unproductive spending and
waste. Such thinkers argue against public investment to comple-
ment private wealth creation. The philosophy of Milton Friedman
has replaced that of John Maynard Keynes. Public investment, as a
result, has been curtailed, to the detriment of us all.

The consequences are readily apparent: The economy is threatened by a greedy, poorly regulated, high-flying marketplace. And,
at the same time, America is crumbling. The raging Mississippi
River crashing through dozens of levees in the aftermath of Hur-
ricane Katrina and overwhelming the city of New Orleans, the
devastating collapse of the Stone Arch bridge in Minneapolis—
these are not isolated incidents, but rather the harbingers of new
disasters. With a reckless complacency, the nation has allowed its
vital infrastructure to deteriorate.

How extensive is this neglect? In a report issued in 2005 the
statistics compiled by the American Society of Civil Engineers
(ASCE) document a grim story, and predict a dangerous future.
Twenty-seven percent of the nation's 590,750 bridges, for example,
are "structurally deficient or functionally obsolete"; repairing these
conditions would cost $9.4 billion a year over the next twenty
years. And yet bridges, according to the Civil Engineers' report,

would require the *least* investment of money and material of all the fifteen categories that their study includes in the nation's infrastructure.

Water facilities need an $11 billion annual investment. An estimated $268 billion will be required to restore schools to "good" condition; in New York City alone, officials complain of $1.7 billion needed for deferred maintenance on eight hundred decaying school buildings. The U.S. Army Corps of Engineers operates more than 12,000 miles of inland waterways, and more than half of the 257 locks on this network are "functionally obsolete." Congestion on the nation's roads and highways is a misery: Americans spend 3.5 billion hours in traffic each year—and this, according to a 2006 House Transportation Committee report, adds up to a cost of $63.2 billion in wasted time and fuel. The bottom line to the ASCE report was cited in the prologue, but it is worth repeating: Over the next five years, to bring America's infrastructure to reasonably safe standards will require a *$1.6 trillion investment.*

Moreover, deterioration promises to worsen as demand for infrastructure services continues to outpace capacity. The more goods and people move about the country by roads, planes, ships, and trains, the greater the investment that will be required to maintain reasonable safety standards. Time is not on our side.

So, what can be done?

The preceding chapters offer, I believe, a general strategy that time after time, generation after generation, has proven to work: innovative public investments are monies well spent, capital expenditures that continue to pay both tangible and intangible dividends.

While these historical examples have helped to shape my philosophy, I am no less a product of my own experiences. I have spent a lifetime as an investment banker. And I have also worked in government—as an ambassador, as a governor of the New York Stock Exchange, and as chairman of New York's Municipal Assistance Corporation. What I have seen and done, the firsthand lessons I learned about the need for farsighted and resourceful government, have also served to inform and guide my response to this critical need.

America requires a new and different approach to selecting, financing, and managing its investments in the country's infrastructure. The country needs a National Infrastructure Bank (NIB).

The NIB would be similar to the World Bank or the European Investment Bank. Funded with an initial capital base of $60 billion, this bank would be empowered to insure the bonds of state and local governments, provide targeted and precise subsidies, and would issue its own thirty- to fifty-year bonds to finance itself with conservative 3:1 gearing. Such an institution could easily provide $250 billion of new capital over the next five years to invest in construction and maintenance projects across the nation— money that would create several million new jobs as a recession deepens. With additional reasonable gearing, significantly higher levels of capital—as much as $1 trillion—could be generated over a five- to seven-year period.

At present, the federal government is spending $73 billion annually on infrastructure projects. But there is no system guiding these funds toward their most important uses. Much is sent to state capitals by formula. Other funds are allocated by tacit agreements between members of Congress and the federal agencies, or even more overtly through "earmark" appropriations—pet patronage projects sponsored by representatives or senators. It is a system that has, notoriously, built multimillion-dollar "bridges to nowhere." The National Infrastructure Bank would put an end to such boondoggle spending.

States and localities would come to the Bank with project applications, and the Bank would evaluate and rank these proposals in a financially disciplined manner on a project-by-project basis. If—and only if—the Bank found the national benefits compelling, then it could involve itself in several essential ways: it could buy credits or enhancements for the project's financing; it could provide interest-rate subsidies or otherwise reduce the borrowers' cost of capital; it could lend directly; or it could finance sinking funds. The National Infrastructure Bank would, like any well-run financial instruction, support those investments that had the prospect of earning returns over the long term.

Fortunately, a bipartisan bill to achieve this end—the National Infrastructure Bank bill of 2007—has already been submitted in the Senate and companion legislation has been proposed in the House. As the nation faces problems it has not seen since the Great Depression, the challenge to the newly elected Congress and administration is to make this job-generating bill into law.

One final question needs to be raised: How would the nation pay for this new infrastructure policy? The first source of funding should come from the funds now dedicated to existing programs; approximately $60 billion annually could be taken from these programs and there still would be a balance remaining. Additionally, taxes and fees that are currently imposed on infrastructure users—for example, port fees, fuel taxes, airline ticket surcharges— would continue to generate revenue.

The nation can increase its investment in the infrastructure and still have fiscal discipline. The tax system can become more efficient and fairer, and at the same time raise revenue for invest- ment purposes; a consumption or value-added tax, and a carbon or energy tax are just two examples of more equitable ways to raise taxpayer revenue.

The fiscal decisions that need to be made are clear. Our nation confronts mass transit strained beyond capacity, planes stranded on tarmacs, roads packed bumper-to-bumper with traffic, waste supply systems threatened in both quantity and quality, crowded ports, and bridges and tunnels that are obsolete. An investment in the country's infrastructure is an investment that will help deter- mine the future quality of American life.

A major, federally assisted infrastructure program is required to make up for the inability of state and local governments to play their traditional role; to improve homeland defense; to generate badly needed jobs for the U.S. economy; and to improve national productivity. The federal government should work with the states to create this vehicle. Every great American president has spon- sored a great investment project; the new administration should continue that record with the present initiative.

All of these issues require an active government working with business and with labor to find solutions, and for Democrats and Republicans in the Congress to cooperate with each other instead of constant opposition and political warfare. Deregulation and faith in the market will not, by themselves, improve the situation.

The National Infrastructure Bank would be subject to all the requirements of a private-sector public company. That would include the accounting standards required by the SEC, as well as disclosure and transparency standards of the most stringent types. The recent financial crisis had its origin in lax enforcement of many of the rules, with disastrous results. Modern market capitalism requires strong ethical standards as well as legal and accounting standards of the highest order. We have seen what happens when these are bypassed.

America today is badly divided. It is divided on very basic and profound issues—on the size and role of our government and its relationship to the citizen, and on the nation's role in the world, and our relationship to friends and foes alike.

Americans want to be positive members of the world community and to exert power responsibly. That was the country I came to in 1942 and that was the country I left in 1997, when President Clinton sent me to France. It is not the country I found upon my return.

I am an American who believes in the Atlantic partnership, in the United Nations and in NATO. I am a Democrat who has regularly voted for a number of Republicans, and I continue to do so. I am also a capitalist and I believe that market capitalism is the best economic system ever invented; but it must be fair, it must be regulated, and it must be ethical. The last few years have shown the excesses that can come about when our system is abused in the service of greed. Only capitalists can kill capitalism. Our system cannot stand much more abuse of the type we have witnessed recently, nor can it stand much more of the financial and social polarization we are seeing today. We are very much on the wrong track.

"The business of this country is business," Calvin Coolidge said. That is still true. But it requires that business and the political leadership remember that the basis of our democracy is fairness. A successful democratic market economy must be seen as fair to the majority of its citizens. This is not the case today in America. As an earlier president, Theodore Roosevelt, warned, "A great democracy must be progressive or it will soon cease to be great or a democracy."

The history of American success is, as the ten examples in this book demonstrate, a narrative shaped by courageous leaders who found the vision to make bold and innovative investments in the country's future. This is a lesson and a call to action that we cannot ignore as we struggle at home and abroad with the complexities of a new century.

AUTHOR'S NOTE

T HE YEAR WAS 1975, and I was a young investment banker making my way on Wall Street, but this particular afternoon I found myself sitting in the wood-paneled private Washington office of a distinguished U.S. senator. Henry "Scoop" Jackson was considering a run for president, and wanted to discuss urban issues.

I was flattered to be the audience for his candid, coolly pragmatic wisdoms on a subject of great interest to me. Suddenly, there was a cautious knock on the door and an aide, looking a bit nonplussed, entered. The senator stared at her in reproof. I told you, he grumbled, I did not want to be disturbed. She nodded meekly, then pointed an accusatory finger at me. I had an important call, she announced.

Apologizing profusely, I stepped outside. My embarrassment

was genuine. What office crisis, I wondered, could demand my immediate attention? I was moving up in Lazard Frères' merger and acquisitions hierarchy and juggling my share of pending deals, but certainly nothing that necessitated an abrupt withdrawal from a meeting with such a respected national figure.

I was wrong. It *was* a remarkable call.

The caller was David Burke, chief of staff of the governor of New York and an old friend, requesting my presence at an urgent meeting with the governor this very afternoon. Yet, these were only minor astonishments. What made the call so disconcerting was the grim news that the governor's chief of staff shared: New York City was on the verge of bankruptcy.

I took the first shuttle back to LaGuardia Airport and on the flight reviewed in my mind what I knew. Intimations of the city's financial crisis had been circulating around Wall Street for months. Only recently, in fact, a broker had called to offer me city bonds that paid 9.25 percent interest, and were triple tax-free to boot; the deal was too good, and in my banker's calculus this was a sure sign the city's future was a perilous investment. No thanks, I told the broker.

Of course, the newspapers were also filled with stories detailing the city's escalating economic predicament. One recent report had revealed that the governor and mayor were going to the White House with the clearly futile yet wishful hope that President Gerald Ford would authorize a $1 billion loan to steady a listing city. But I had never truly appreciated how rough the financial waters were, or how truly close to sinking the city was. It had never occurred to me that municipal bankruptcy was a viable option, let alone a distinct and rapidly approaching possibility.

As the plane descended over the island of Manhattan, I looked down on the bustling, crowded city that, after my family had escaped from the Holocaust in Europe, had become my home. I gazed at the towers shimmering in the early afternoon sun and felt an immigrant's pride in having been able to make my way in this gilded metropolis; and I also felt an immense gratitude to the country and to the city that had taken me in.

My mind racing, I did a quick inventory of what the city's bankruptcy would mean. It wasn't simply that bills would not be paid, that police, firemen, sanitation people, health workers, and teachers would not know when they would receive their next paycheck. No less significant, it meant that the funds necessary for the upkeep of the city—its roadways, bridges, airports, schools, and libraries—would also be frozen. A great city would deteriorate. The daily hardships would be deeply felt by families throughout the five boroughs; and the economic and cultural consequences would reverberate across the nation and, possibly, throughout the world.

By the time I arrived at the governor's surprisingly small, cave-like midtown office, I had made up my mind. It would be unacceptable—intolerable, in fact—for the city to go broke. I would do whatever I could to try to help prevent such a disaster.

I had never met Governor Hugh Carey before. But as if to emphasize the looming emergency, there was no time now for pleasantries. Without even a brief prelude, the governor launched into a daunting recitation of the bills that would too soon be due. It appeared, he concluded, that within a month the city would be forced to file for bankruptcy. After that, it would only be a matter of time before the state would have little choice but to seek similar relief.

I told Governor Carey that in my opinion, bankruptcy was not an option; it would destroy the city. He could count on whatever knowledge and energies I could bring to the fight to work out an alternative solution. I also made it clear that I had no experience with municipal government. The challenges were too financially intricate and politically complex for me to take them on single-handedly. I suggested he appoint a bipartisan team to advise him. With little hesitation, the governor agreed that he would recruit two Republicans and another Democrat to work with us.

There was, however, one restraint on the formal announcement of my participation in any attempt to rescue the city. Before I could officially begin work, I needed to receive the permission of my firm's senior partner, André Meyer.

Mr. Meyer (as I always called him) was in poor health, so I went uptown to his apartment in the Carlyle Hotel to meet with him. For bankers of my generation, Mr. Meyer was a vaunted, legendary, and, truth be told, intimidating figure. Sitting across from him in his elegant apartment high above the city, the two of us surrounded by his magnificent pictures—Picassos, Renoirs, Gauguins, and Monets glowing on the walls—his authority and eminence seemed to be reinforced. We were soon joined by Judge Simon Rifkind, counsel to our firm, and a man, I knew, of considerable wisdom. For a moment, I panicked. I thought Mr. Meyer would never agree that I—and by extension the firm—should become entangled in such a hapless enterprise. Still, I made my case, emphasizing that the consequences of the city's default would not simply be felt in New York but would rock the international marketplace.

When I was done, Mr. Meyer considered my argument; and

then, with an obvious reluctance, he agreed to my signing on for what he rather disdainfully predicted would become a very visible role. Judge Rifkind concurred. The city needed help, he emphasized.

In his wry, Gallic way, Mr. Meyer also offered a word of caution. "Public service," he said, "is like having a young mistress. You should be careful. It's tempting."

With absolute certainty, I told Mr. Meyer my role would be temporary. I would devote a few weeks—three, four at most—to helping the city, and then I would return full time to my responsibilities at the firm. Mr. Meyer's response was simply a tight, knowing smile.

And so I threw myself into the task. Working with the governor's three other appointees and with the support of the mayor, the City Council, and the state legislature, we created the Emergency Financial Control Board (EFCB) and the Municipal Assistance Corporation (MAC). Essentially, the EFCB was an accountant's mechanism, a way to regulate spending and, in time, balance the budget. MAC was a more complicated and powerful institution. It functioned, in effect, as a bank. MAC would collect the city's sales taxes and stock transfer taxes and, using these revenues as guarantees, would then issue its own bonds.

For a while, it was rough going. The city lurched from crisis to crisis. But bankruptcy was averted. New York City was saved from default. And soon things started to change.

By 1981, thanks in large part to the EFCB and MAC, the city had balanced its budget. Four years later, MAC no longer had any need to sell bonds; the city was able to sell its own. And by 2008, all of the outstanding MAC bonds had been paid off. Today, New

York City has full access to the financial markets and can borrow to accommodate all of its needs. In the ensuing decades of balanced budgets—even frequent surpluses—New York and its residents have prospered. The city has become preeminent, acclaimed as the economic and cultural capital of the world.

There were, however, two consequences I had not foreseen when I met with the governor that sobering afternoon in 1975. First, André Meyer was correct. My association with MAC turned out not to be as brief as I had anticipated. I served eighteen years. Further, the attraction to public service, as Mr. Myer had also slyly predicted, was indeed "tempting." In 1997, President Clinton appointed me ambassador to France.

NEARLY FORTY YEARS HAVE passed since I was a banker immersed in a complex and potentially disastrous municipal economic crisis. The world (and I, too, for certain) has changed over the hectic course of those decades. Yet once again it is a time of grave economic crisis—only now the trauma is national in scope. And, as I had predicted when I joined the battle to guide a nearly bankrupt New York City back to solvency, a moribund economy leads to the collapse of the infrastructure.

The central thesis of this book, therefore, is in many ways a product of the experiences I had as a younger man. In fact, my interest in infrastructure began after World War II when I observed the reconstruction of Europe and was fascinated by its leaders, such as Jean Monnet. They were innovators who invested boldly in public infrastructure and built modern highways and high-speed rail to make devastated regions competitive again.

I remembered these efforts in the seventies as I saw the dilapidated state of many American schools and the overall despair in our older cities. As chairman of MAC, I urged investment in new school construction and won the support of the unions to get it done. It was my years helping to run MAC that shaped my philosophy.

It is a premise of this narrative that the activist economic principles, the cooperation of business and labor, and the bipartisan political cooperation that were used so successfully to rescue New York are both relevant and, I contend, necessary if the country is effectively going to confront two new crises: a besieged economy and a national infrastructure that is too old and decrepit to function effectively in the twenty-first century.

AS I HAVE MADE clear, this book—and its underlying thesis—has also been shaped by my love for history. To develop my argument and to document the ten case studies, I have largely relied on the works of other, more traditional historians. Therefore, I not only want to acknowledge their invaluable contributions to the book, but also to offer up some of the sources I consulted with the greatest frequency to any reader interested in digging deeper into specific areas.

LOUISIANA PURCHASE:

François Barbé-Marbois. *The History of Louisiana*. Philadelphia: Carey & Lea, 1830.

Charles A. Cerami. *Jefferson's Great Gamble: The Remarkable Story of Jefferson Napoleon and the Men Behind the Louisiana Purchase.* Naperville: Source Books, 2003.

Alexander DeConde. *This Affair of Louisiana.* New York: Charles Scribner's Sons, 1976.

The Count de las Cases. *Memoirs of the Life, Exile and Conversation of the Emperor Napoleon, Vol. I.* New York: Redfield, 1885.

Susan Dunn. *Jefferson's Second Revolution: The Election Crisis of 1800 and the Triumph of Republicanism.* New York: Houghton Mifflin Books, 2004.

Thomas J. Fleming. *The Louisiana Purchase.* New Jersey: John Wiley and Sons, 2003.

P. L. Ford, ed. *The Writings of Thomas Jefferson,* Vol. IX. Washington, D.C., 1903.

Joseph Harris. "Westward Ho!" *Smithsonian Magazine,* April 2003.

Henry Howe. *Historical Collections of the Great West.* Cincinnati: E. Morgan & Co., 1851.

Thomas Jefferson. *The Writings of Thomas Jefferson,* Vol. VIII. New York: G. P. Putnam's Sons, 1897.

Ralph Louis Ketcham. *James Madison: A Biography.* Charlottesville: University of Virginia Press, 1990.

Jon Kukla. *A Wilderness So Immense: The Louisiana Purchase and the Destiny of America.* New York: Anchor Books, 2004.

E. Wilson Lyon. *Louisiana in French Diplomacy, 1759–1804.* Norman: University of Oklahoma Press, 1934.

ERIE CANAL:

Peter L. Bernstein. *Wedding of the Waters: The Erie Canal and the Making of a Great Nation.* New York: W. W. Norton and Company, 2005.

Cadwallader D. Colden. *Memoirs at the Celebration of the Completion of the New York Canals.* New York: W. A. Davis, 1825.

Evan Cornog. *The Birth of Empire: DeWitt Clinton and the American Experience, 1769–1828.* New York: Oxford University Press, 1998.

Carter Goodrich. *Canals and American Economic Development.* New York: Columbia University Press, 1961.

David Hosack. *Memoir of DeWitt Clinton.* New York: J. Seymour, 1829.

Laws of the State of New York in Relation to the Erie and Champlain Canals. Albany, 1825.

Henry O'Reilly. *Settlement in the West: Sketches of Rochester.* Rochester: W. Alling, 1838.

Lois Kimball Matthews Rosenberry. *The Erie Canal and the Settlement of the West.* Buffalo: Buffalo Historical Society Press, 1910.

Noble E. Whitford. *History of the Canal System of the State of New York,* Vol. I, Albany, 1906.

TRANSCONTINENTAL RAILROAD:

Stephen E. Ambrose. *Nothing Like It in the World.* New York: Simon & Schuster, 2000. Note: This chapter relies extensively on Ambrose's definitive and engaging book.

David Haward Bain. *Empire Express: Building the First Transcontinental Railroad.* New York: Penguin, 1967.

Harold Evans. *They Made America: From the Steam Engine to the Search Engine: Two Centuries of Innovators.* New York: Little Brown & Company, 2004.

Abraham Lincoln, Don Edward Fehrenbacher, ed. *Speeches and Writings, 1832–1858.* New York: Library of America, 1989.

Transcript, "Transcontinental Railroad," Public Broadcasting Service, WGBH Educational Foundation, 2003.

LAND GRANT COLLEGES:

Coy F. Cross. *Justin Smith Morrill: Father of the Land-Grant Colleges.* East Lansing: Michigan State University Press, 1999.

Frank Burt Freidel. *America in the Twentieth Century.* New York: Knopf, 1970.

Randal Leigh Hoyer. *The Gentleman from Vermont: The Career of Justin S. Morrill in the United States House of Representatives.* East Lansing: Michigan State University, 1974.

Thomas Jefferson. "Sixth State of the Nation." Washington, D.C., Dec. 2, 1806.

A. C. McLaughlin. *Higher Education in Michigan.* Lansing, 1891.

Justin Smith Morrill. "Morrill Legislation Debate of 1858." *Congressional Globe,* April 20, 1858.

Andrew D. White. "The Need for Another University." *Forum* 6, January 1889.

HOMESTEAD ACT:

Frank Tracy Carlton. *Organized Labor in American History.* New York: D. Appleton and Company, 1920.

Benjamin Horace Hibbard. *A History of Public Land Policies.* Madison: University of Wisconsin Press, 1965.

Register of Debates, 19th Congress, 1st Session; 26th Congress, 2nd Session. Library of Congress.

Lucy E. Parson. *The Life of Albert R. Parsons, with a Brief History of the Labor Movement in America.* Boston: Adamant Media Corp., 2001.

James D. Richardson. *James Buchanan: A Compilation of the Messages and Papers of the Presidents.* Whitefish: Kessinger Publishing, 2004.

Fred A. Shannon. "The Homestead Act and the Labor Surplus," *American Historical Review,* July 1936.

Hans L. Trefousse. *Andrew Johnson: A Biography.* New York: W. W. Norton and Company, 1989.

PANAMA CANAL:

David McCullough. *The Path Between the Seas: The Creation of the Panama Canal 1870–1914.* New York: Simon & Schuster, 1977.

Patricia O'Toole. *When Trumpets Call: Theodore Roosevelt After the White House.* New York: Simon & Schuster, 2006.

Theodore Roosevelt, *Address to the Assembled Panama Canal Force.* Panama: 1906.

REA:

Deward Clayton Brown. *Electricity for Rural America: The Fight for the REA*. Westport, Conn.: Greenwood Press, 1980.

Congressional Record, 74th Congress.

Co-op Currents. "How Rural Co-ops Transformed the Countryside." East Montpelier, Vt.: Washington Electric Cooperative, October, 2004.

Albert Fried. *FDR and His Enemies.* New York: St. Martin's Press, 1999.

Harold L. Ickes. *The Secret Diary of Harold L. Ickes,* Vol. I. New York: Simon & Schuster, 1954.

Theodore Roosevelt. *Presidential Addresses and State Papers and European Addresses: December 8, 1908 to June 7, 1910.* Whitefish: Kessinger Publishing, 2006.

RFC:

Philip Abbott. *The Exemplary Presidency: Franklin D. Roosevelt and the American Political Tradition.* Amherst: University of Massachusetts Press, 1990.

Robert B. Anderson. *Final Reports on the Reconstruction Finance Corporation.* Washington: U.S. Government Printing Office, 1959.

David Burner. *Herbert Hoover: A Public Life.* New York: Alfred A. Knopf, 1979.

Wilton Eckley. *Herbert Hoover.* Boston: Twayne Publishers, 1990.

Joseph Huthmacher and Warren I. Susman, eds. *Herbert Hoover and the Crisis of American Capitalism.* Cambridge, Mass.: Schenkman Publishing Company, 1973.

James Stuart Olson. *Herbert Hoover and the Reconstruction Finance Corporation, 1931–1933.* Ames: Iowa State University Press, 1977.

James Stuart Olson. *Saving Capitalism: The Reconstruction Finance Corporation and the New Deal, 1933–1940.* Princeton, N.J.: Princeton University Press, 1980.

Elliott Roosevelt and James Brough. *A Rendezvous with Destiny: The Roosevelts of the White House.* New York: G. P. Putnam's Sons, 1975.

Gene Smith. *The Shattered Dream: Herbert Hoover and the Great Depression.* New York: William Morrow & Company, 1970.

THE G.I. BILL:

Stephen Ambrose. *NewsHour,* PBS. July 4, 2000.

Doris Kearns Goodwin. *No Ordinary Time: Franklin and Eleanor Roosevelt: The Home Front in World War II.* New York: Simon & Schuster, 1995.

John Grafton, ed. *Great Speeches: Franklin Delano Roosevelt.* New York: Dover Publications, 1998.

Suzanne Mettler. "The Creation of the G.I. Bill of Rights of 1944: Melding Social and Participatory Citizenship Ideals," *Journal of Policy History,* 17, November 4, 2005.

———. *Soldiers to Citizens: The G.I. Bill and the Making of the Greatest Generation.* New York: Oxford University Press, 2005.

INTERSTATE HIGHWAYS:

Dwight D. Eisenhower. *At Ease: Stories I Tell to Friends.* New York: Doubleday & Co., 1967.

Stephen B. Goodard. *Getting There: The Epic Struggle Between Road and Rail in the American Century.* New York: Basic Books/HarperCollins, 1994.

Tom Lewis. *Divided Highways.* New York: Penguin Group, 1997.

Lee Mertz. "Origins of the Interstate." Federal Highway Administration, U.S. Department of Transportation. http://www.fhwa.dot.gov/infrastructure/origin.htm.

Bill Redeker. "Interstate Highway System at a Crossroads: A Crumbling Legacy." *ABC News,* June 29, 2006.

ACKNOWLEDGMENTS

I WOULD LIKE TO THANK Bill Barrett and Howard Blum for their help in the writing and editing of this book. I also would like to acknowledge the contribution of my brilliant research assistants at the Rohatyn Center for International Affairs at Middlebury College, Ioana Literat and Sara Lowes. Ms. Literat devoted long hours and great skill to helping research and organize early drafts of a number of chapters. I also owe a debt of gratitude to Charlotte Tate, assistant director of the Rohatyn Center, who oversaw the work of Ms. Literat and Ms. Lowes and made sure it did not interfere with their academic studies. Allison Stanger at Middlebury also gave invaluable support to the project. I would be remiss if I didn't thank Lynn Nesbit, my agent, for her support and

Alice Mayhew, my editor, for her editorial wisdom, and Roger Labrie, whose assistance was invaluable.

I also appreciate the invaluable assistance and insight of Caitlin Klevorick, who reviewed the chapters and provided additional research, annotation of sources, and editorial comment. In addition, I am grateful to Maura Pally for so thoroughly fact-checking the completed manuscript. Everett Ehrlich was a wise and trusted counsel throughout the writing. Finally, I want to thank my assistant, Elizabeth Davies, who prepared the various versions of the text and provided editorial suggestions as well.

INDEX

Index

ABOUT THE AUTHOR

Felix Rohatyn, a frequent contributor to *The New York Review of Books,* was a managing director at the investment banking firm Lazard Freres & Co. LLC and served as the U.S. ambassador to France. From 1975 to 1993, Mr. Rohatyn was chairman of the Municipal Assistance Corporation of the State of New York, where he managed the negotiations that enabled New York City to resolve its financial crisis.